WILLIAMS-SONOMA

PASTA

RECIPES AND TEXT
ERICA DE MANE

GENERAL EDITOR
CHUCK WILLIAMS

PHOTOGRAPHS
MAREN CARUSO

SIMON & SCHUSTER • SOURCE

NEW YORK • LONDON • TORONTO • SYDNEY • SINGAPORE

CONTENTS

SPRING AND SUMMER

AUTUMN AND WINTER

HEARTY VEGETARIAN

INTRODUCTION

Using a bounty of fresh herbs, vibrant spices, rich cheeses, and olive oils to create wonderful depth of flavor, the pasta dishes in this cookbook harken back to Italian home cooking. Old-World cooks know that carefully choosing the best ingredients and enjoying the time you spend in the kitchen is what makes the most memorable meals. The endless variety of pasta is revealed in these pages—there are string pastas and filled pastas, pasta soups and baked lasagnes, hearty meat and fresh vegetable dishes.

Whether you want to make a pasta from the fresh vegetables in season, impress your dinner guests with something unusual, or re-create a favorite classic, you'll find just the recipe you need. Each recipe in this book is kitchen-tested and highlights a particular ingredient, term, or technique, and a chapter of basics in the back of the book offers a comprehensive overview of pasta making. I hope you'll use a recipe from this book to make pasta for dinner tonight!

THE CLASSICS

Classics are classics for good reason: Everybody loves them. Some iconic pasta dishes have evolved over the years to suit changing tastes and trends. It's rewarding to return to the original recipes: linguine with clams in the style of the Amalfi coast, true pasta carbonara, or a rich, slow-simmered Bolognese ragù on egg pasta.

PASTA WITH HOME-STYLE TOMATO SAUCE

TOMATO SAUCE VARIATIONS

Toss this versatile tomato sauce with pasta or use it in a baked pasta dish (see Baked Ziti with Tomatoes, Ricotta, and Mozzarella, page 98). You can vary the flavor by adding chopped prosciutto or salami, olives, capers, toasted pine nuts, or a splash of cream at the last minute. Or experiment with different herbs: marjoram, oregano, savory, mint, or tarragon can replace the basil or the parsley. The mixture of fresh and canned tomatoes gives the sauce a pleasantly chunky texture.

In a large frying pan over medium heat, warm the ¼ cup olive oil. Add the prosciutto end (if using), the onion, carrot, leek, and celery and sauté until just turning lightly golden, about 8 minutes. Add the garlic and sauté without coloring, about 1 minute. Add the fresh and canned tomatoes with juice, bay leaf, and thyme sprigs. Season with salt and pepper to taste and cook, uncovered, until slightly thickened, no more than 20 minutes. The sauce should remain at a lively simmer; stir several times during cooking.

Meanwhile, bring a large pot of water to a boil. Generously salt the boiling water, add the pasta, and cook until al dente, 7–9 minutes.

Remove the prosciutto end (if used), thyme sprigs, and bay leaf and discard. Add the parsley, basil, and a drizzle of olive oil. Taste and adjust the seasoning.

Drain the pasta and put it in a warmed large, shallow bowl. Add the sauce, toss it gently with the pasta, garnish with thyme sprigs, and serve immediately.

Cooking Tip: To thicken the sauce quickly and preserve its bright color and fresh taste, use a wide, shallow frying pan so the liquid can evaporate without long cooking.

MAKES 4 MAIN-COURSE OR 6 FIRST-COURSE SERVINGS

¼ cup (2 fl oz/60 ml) extra-virgin olive oil, plus extra for drizzling

1 small chunk fatty prosciutto end (optional)

1 onion, finely diced

1 carrot, peeled and finely diced

1 leek, white part only, finely diced

1 small inner celery stalk, finely diced

3 cloves garlic, thinly sliced

4 fresh plum (Roma) tomatoes, peeled and seeded (page 93), then diced

1 can (35 oz/1.1 kg) plum (Roma) tomatoes, chopped, with juice

1 bay leaf

2 or 3 fresh thyme sprigs, plus several sprigs for garnish

Salt and pepper

1 lb (500 g) sturdy pasta such as spaghetti, bucatini, or dried shaped pasta

Small handful of fresh flat-leaf (Italian) parsley leaves, coarsely chopped

About 10 fresh basil leaves, coarsely chopped

FETTUCCINE ALFREDO

1½ cups (12 fl oz/375 ml) heavy (double) cream

5 tablespoons (2½ oz/75 g) unsalted butter

1 cup (4 oz/125 g) grated Parmesan cheese

Salt and freshly ground pepper

Freshly grated nutmeg

1 lb (500 g) homemade tagliatelle (pages 107–8) or purchased fresh fettuccine

Bring a large pot of water to a boil. Meanwhile, in a large saucepan over high heat, bring the cream and butter to a boil. Reduce the heat to low and simmer for about 1 minute. Add 6 tablespoons of the grated Parmesan and whisk over low heat until smooth, about 1 minute longer. Remove from the heat and season with salt and pepper to taste and a generous pinch of nutmeg. (Be judicious with the salt. The Parmesan is itself salty, and too much added salt will throw this creamy, sweet sauce out of balance.)

Generously salt the boiling water, add the pasta, and cook until al dente, 1–3 minutes, depending on the freshness of the pasta. Drain the pasta well.

Put the pasta in a warmed large, shallow bowl. Pour on the sauce and sprinkle with 6 more tablespoons of the cheese. Toss well. Serve immediately. Pass the remaining cheese at the table.

Serving Tip: In Italy, this luxurious dish is served in small portions as a first course. Try it before a simple main dish of poached or baked fish or grilled meat.

MAKES 4 MAIN-COURSE OR 6 FIRST-COURSE SERVINGS

CLASSIC ALFREDO INGREDIENTS

The success of this Roman dish depends on first-rate ingredients. If you can find an unsalted European-style butter, such as Keller's (widely available at gourmet groceries), use it here. It has a richer flavor and a lower water content than everyday brands. Seek out a nonultrapasteurized heavy cream for the best taste. When you buy a chunk of Parmesan, ask the clerk to cut a wedge fresh from a wheel, to make sure it is not too dried out.

SPAGHETTI ALLA CARBONARA

Bring a large pot of water to a boil. Meanwhile, break the eggs into a warmed large, shallow bowl, add the cheeses, and whisk to blend well.

Generously salt the boiling water, add the spaghetti, and cook until al dente, 7–9 minutes.

While the pasta is cooking, in a large frying pan over medium heat, warm the olive oil. Add the pancetta and sauté until just starting to become crisp, about 4 minutes. Add the garlic and sauté for 1 minute. Add the white wine and cook until reduced by half.

Drain the pasta, leaving a bit of water clinging to it, and add it to the bowl. Toss quickly (this will heat the eggs and leave a creamy coating on each strand of pasta). Add the pancetta with all of the pan juices. Season with salt to taste and a generous amount of pepper. Add the parsley and toss again. Serve immediately.

Note: This dish includes egg that is only partially cooked. For more information, see page 113.

MAKES 4 MAIN-COURSE OR 6 FIRST-COURSE SERVINGS

PANCETTA

Only pancetta, the cured but unsmoked Italian bacon, should be used in this famous pasta dish from Rome. Pancetta is made from the same cut, pork belly, as the more common bacon, but it is salt-cured instead of smoked, giving it a subtler taste. Smoked bacon will overpower the delicate flavors of this dish. Look for good domestic brands of pancetta at delicatessens and Italian markets.

2 eggs, at room temperature

¼ cup (1 oz/30 g) grated pecorino romano cheese

¼ cup (1 oz/30 g) grated Parmesan cheese

1 lb (500 g) spaghetti

¼ cup (2 fl oz/60 ml) extra-virgin olive oil

¼-lb (125-g) piece pancetta, cut into small cubes

2 cloves garlic, very thinly sliced

½ cup (4 fl oz/125 ml) dry white wine

Salt and coarsely ground pepper

Generous handful of fresh flat-leaf (Italian) parsley leaves, coarsely chopped

PASTA CAPRESE

5 large tomatoes

½ cup (4 fl oz/125 ml) extra-virgin olive oil

1 teaspoon balsamic vinegar

2 cloves garlic, very thinly sliced (see Note)

Salt and freshly ground black pepper

Pinch of cayenne pepper

1 lb (500 g) penne or ziti

½ lb (250 g) fresh mozzarella cheese, cut into small cubes

About 15 fresh basil leaves, finely shredded, plus several sprigs

Peel and seed the tomatoes (page 93), then cut them into small dice. Drain the diced tomatoes in a colander for about 15 minutes to remove excess liquid.

In a bowl, combine the drained tomatoes, olive oil, vinegar, and garlic. Season to taste with salt and black pepper and the cayenne. Toss and let sit at room temperature for about 20 minutes to develop the flavor.

Meanwhile, bring a large pot of water to a boil over high heat. Generously salt the boiling water, add the pasta, and cook until al dente, 10–12 minutes.

Drain the pasta and put it in a warmed large, shallow bowl. Add the tomato mixture and toss. Add the mozzarella and basil shreds and toss gently. The heat from the pasta will start to melt the cheese. Taste and adjust the seasoning. Garnish with basil sprigs and serve at once.

Note: Look for firm garlic cloves without any evidence of green sprouts. If a sprout is visible, be sure to cut it away before slicing the clove. These green shoots would impart an unwelcome sharp flavor to this uncooked sauce.

MAKES 4 MAIN-COURSE OR 6 FIRST-COURSE SERVINGS

FRESH MOZZARELLA

In its fresh form, mozzarella cheese should be soft, almost spongy, with a gentle milky tang. In Italy, mozzarella was originally made from the milk of water buffaloes, but today much of it is made with cow's milk. Freshly made cow's milk mozzarella is sold at many well-stocked supermarkets and Italian grocers. Imported buffalo's milk mozzarella is also sometimes available, but it is often not as fresh as it should be. Ask when the cheese was shipped, or better yet, ask to taste a piece. The flavor will be tangier than the cow's milk variety, but it should never taste sour.

SPAGHETTI WITH MEATBALLS

To make the meatballs, in a large bowl, combine the bread crumbs and milk and mix well. Add the sausage, beef, egg, ricotta, one-third of the Parmesan, shallot, spices, a good sprinkling of marjoram, and 1 garlic clove, minced. Mix briefly with your hands just until the ingredients are well distributed. Season well with salt and pepper. Form the mixture into small balls ½–1 inch (12 mm–2.5 cm) in diameter. In a large frying pan over medium heat, pour in the olive oil to a depth of ¼ inch (6 mm). When it is hot, add the meatballs (in batches, if necessary) and brown well on all sides. Transfer to a tray lined with paper towels to drain.

Discard the oil in the frying pan and wipe out any burned bits. In the pan over medium heat, warm 3 tablespoons olive oil and sauté the onion until soft and lightly golden, about 4 minutes. Slice and add the remaining 2 garlic cloves and sauté about 1 minute longer. Add the wine and let simmer until it is almost completely evaporated. Chop the tomatoes and add them along with their juice. Then add the stock and bay leaf and season to taste with salt and pepper. Reduce the heat to medium-low and simmer, uncovered, until slightly thickened, about 10 minutes. Add the meatballs, reduce the heat to low, and let simmer, uncovered, until the meatballs are cooked through, 5–8 minutes.

Meanwhile, bring a large pot of water to a boil. Generously salt the boiling water, add the pasta, and cook until al dente, 7–9 minutes. Drain the pasta and put it in a warmed large, shallow bowl. Add a sprinkling of chopped marjoram to the sauce and pour it over the pasta. Drizzle the pasta with olive oil and toss gently. Garnish with the marjoram sprigs and serve immediately. Pass the remaining Parmesan at the table.

MAKES 4 MAIN-COURSE SERVINGS

¼ cup (½ oz/15 g) coarse fresh bread crumbs

¼ cup (2 fl oz/60 ml) milk

½ lb (250 g) pork sausage, casings removed

¾ lb (375 g) ground (minced) beef

1 egg

½ cup (4 oz/125 g) ricotta cheese

1½ cups (6 oz/185 g) grated Parmesan cheese

1 large shallot, minced

Pinch *each* of ground nutmeg and cloves

Fresh marjoram leaves, chopped, plus whole sprigs

3 cloves garlic

Salt and pepper

Olive oil, as needed

1 yellow onion, diced

¼ cup (2 fl oz/60 ml) dry white wine

1 large can (35 oz/1.1 kg) plus 1 small can (12 oz/375 g) plum (Roma) tomatoes

¼ cup (2 fl oz/60 ml) chicken stock

1 bay leaf

1 lb (500 g) spaghetti

LINGUINE WITH CLAM SAUCE

2 lb (1 kg) very small clams or tiny cockles, scrubbed

½ cup (4 fl oz/125 ml) dry white wine

1 lb (500 g) linguine, spaghetti, or other string pasta

½ cup (4 fl oz/125 ml) extra-virgin olive oil

4 cloves garlic, thinly sliced

Juice of 1 lemon

Generous pinch of red pepper flakes

Salt and freshly ground black pepper

Large handful of fresh flat-leaf (Italian) parsley leaves, coarsely chopped

Bring a large pot of water to a boil. Meanwhile, put the clams in a large saucepan or pot, discarding any that do not close to the touch. Add the white wine, turn the heat to medium-high, and cook, stirring the clams occasionally, until they start to open, 2–3 minutes. Pull each clam from the pot as it opens and place in a large bowl (some take longer than others; if you leave them all in the pot, the early openers will be overcooked). Discard any clams that do not open. Strain the clam broth through a fine-mesh sieve lined with cheesecloth (muslin) into a bowl and set aside.

Generously salt the boiling water, add the pasta, and cook until al dente, 7–9 minutes.

Meanwhile, in a large frying pan over medium-low heat, warm the olive oil. Add the garlic and sauté until very lightly golden. Add the reserved clam broth and lemon juice and simmer over low heat until slightly reduced, about 4 minutes. Add the red pepper flakes and black pepper to taste. Taste the sauce and add a pinch of salt, if necessary.

Drain the pasta well and add it to the frying pan. Add the clams in their shells and any juices that may have accumulated. Toss well over low heat for about 1 minute to coat the pasta. Transfer to a warmed large, shallow bowl, add the parsley, and toss gently. Serve immediately.

Variation Tip: For a classic red clam sauce, reduce the olive oil to ⅓ cup (3 fl oz/80 ml). After sautéing the garlic, add 3 large tomatoes, peeled and seeded (page 93), then chopped. Simmer for about 5 minutes before adding the reserved clam broth.

MAKES 4 MAIN-COURSE OR 6 FIRST-COURSE SERVINGS

SELECTING CLAMS

The best clams for this classic pasta are Manila clams or littlenecks. Pick the smallest ones you can find; they are the most tender. Tiny New Zealand cockles are now widely available in fish markets and are another excellent choice. They result in a more delicately flavored sauce, however. To boost the flavor of the finished sauce, add a few chopped anchovies to the pasta along with the sauce.

BOLOGNESE SAUCE
WITH FRESH EGG PASTA

SOFFRITTO

What sets Bolognese sauce apart from other long-simmered Italian meat sauces is in part the absence of garlic. But it gets flavor from a *soffritto,* sautéed finely chopped aromatic vegetables, in this case onion, carrots, and celery. Garlic, fennel, and pancetta may be added to this mixture for other dishes. Cooking the *soffritto* gently until the vegetables are golden and fragrant will bring out all their natural sugars and add wonderful flavor to a dish.

Cut the onion, carrot, and celery into small dice. Peel and seed the tomatoes (page 93), then finely chop them.

In a Dutch oven or large, heavy flameproof casserole dish over medium-low heat, melt 2 tablespoons of the butter with the olive oil. Add the pancetta and sauté until just starting to crisp, about 3 minutes. Add the onion, carrot, and celery and sauté until aromatic and very lightly golden, 8–10 minutes. Add the ground beef, pork, and veal, stir to break up, season with salt and pepper to taste, and add a generous pinch of nutmeg. Raise the heat to medium and sauté until the meat is lightly browned. (The meat will first release some liquid; after this evaporates, it will begin to brown.) Add the wine and simmer until it is almost completely evaporated. Add the stock and cook until reduced by half. Add the tomatoes, sage, and bay leaf. Reduce the heat to low, cover, and simmer for about 1½ hours, stirring occasionally. If the sauce seems thin, cook it, uncovered, until thick and fragrant, about 10 minutes. Skim the surface of excess fat. Add the cream. Taste and adjust the seasoning.

Bring a large pot of water to a boil. Generously salt the boiling water, add the pasta, and cook until al dente, 1–3 minutes, depending on the freshness of the pasta. Drain and put in a warmed large, shallow bowl. Add the remaining 2 tablespoons butter and 2 tablespoons of the cheese. Toss until the butter melts. Add the sauce and toss again gently. Serve immediately. Pass the remaining cheese at the table.

Note: Like many long-cooked sauces, this one gains flavor if made a few hours or a day ahead and reheated.

MAKES 4 MAIN-COURSE OR 6 FIRST-COURSE SERVINGS

1 large yellow onion

1 carrot, peeled

1 celery stalk

2 large tomatoes

4 tablespoons (2 oz/60 g) unsalted butter

2 tablespoons extra-virgin olive oil

3 thin slices pancetta, finely chopped

½ lb (250 g) *each* ground (minced) beef, pork, and veal

Salt and pepper

Freshly grated nutmeg

½ cup (4 fl oz/125 ml) dry white wine

2 cups (16 fl oz/500 ml) light meat stock (page 111) or beef stock

5 fresh sage leaves

1 bay leaf

⅓ cup (3 fl oz/80 ml) heavy (double) cream

1 lb (500 g) homemade tagliatelle (pages 107–8) or purchased fresh fettuccine

1 cup (4 oz/125 g) grated Parmesan cheese

PASTA WITH GENOESE PESTO, GREEN BEANS, AND POTATOES

FOR THE GENOESE PESTO:

¼ cup (1¼ oz/37 g) pine nuts

¼ cup (1 oz/30 g) walnuts

1 clove garlic

2 cups (2 oz/60 g) loosely packed fresh basil leaves

½ cup (4 fl oz/125 ml) extra-virgin olive oil

½ cup (2 oz/60 g) grated Parmesan cheese

Salt

1 lb (500 g) gemelli or fusilli

1 large boiling potato, peeled and cut into small dice

¼ lb (125 g) green beans, trimmed and halved crosswise

Bring a large pot of water to a boil. Meanwhile, make the pesto: In a blender or a food processor, combine the nuts and garlic. Process to chop coarsely. Add the basil and olive oil and process to a coarse paste. Add the cheese and process briefly, just to incorporate it. The pesto should be fairly smooth but still have some texture. Season with salt to taste.

Generously salt the boiling water, add the pasta and potato, and cook until the pasta is al dente and the potato is tender, 10–12 minutes. During the last 3 minutes of cooking, add the green beans. Drain the pasta, potato, and beans, reserving about ½ cup (4 fl oz/125 ml) of the pasta water. Put the pasta, potato, and beans in a warmed large, shallow bowl. Add a large dollop of the pesto (don't add it all at once, as you may not need it all). Add a few tablespoons of the reserved pasta water to loosen the sauce. Toss well. The pesto should be creamy and coat the pasta well, with little excess. Add more pesto as needed and toss again. Serve immediately.

Note: Use leftover pesto the next day as a sauce for fish or chicken, to toss into a dish of sautéed vegetables such as zucchini (courgettes) or eggplant (aubergine), or to dress a summer tomato salad. To store leftover pesto, smooth the surface, cover with a thin layer of olive oil, wrap, and refrigerate; it will keep for 2–3 days.

MAKES 4 MAIN-COURSE OR 6 FIRST-COURSE SERVINGS

GENOESE PESTO

Made with fresh basil and pine nuts, Genoese pesto is the best-known pesto outside of Italy. It is hard to give exact measurements for the sauce, for although the ingredients are widely agreed upon, the proportions are a matter of taste. This pesto recipe results in a light, herbal pesto with just a hint of garlic. Some people may wish to add more garlic or more cheese, or substitute milder pecorino romano cheese for half of the Parmesan.

QUICK SUPPERS

With a well-stocked pantry, you can throw together a great weeknight pasta dinner in a matter of minutes. Keep some key items on hand: canned tomatoes, good olive oil, dried Italian pasta, anchovies, olives, and a grating cheese or two. If you lack the exact ingredients called for, think of it as a chance to improvise.

PENNE ARRABBIATA

Bring a large pot of water to a boil. Meanwhile, in a large frying pan over low heat, warm the ¼ cup olive oil. Add the garlic and sauté just until it starts to color, about 1 minute. Add the red pepper flakes and sauté for 1 minute. Add the tomatoes with their juice, raise the heat to medium-high, and cook uncovered, stirring occasionally, until the sauce has thickened, about 15 minutes. Season with salt to taste.

Generously salt the boiling water, add the pasta, and cook until al dente, 10–12 minutes. Drain well. Put the pasta in a warmed large, shallow bowl and pour on the tomato sauce. Add the basil and marjoram, drizzle with olive oil, and toss. Serve immediately.

Variation Tip: To make a classic puttanesca sauce, add 3 or 4 minced anchovy fillets, ¼ cup (2 oz/60 g) capers, and ½ cup (2½ oz/ 75 g) pitted black olives to the above sauce when it has finished cooking. Simmer for 1 minute over low heat to blend the flavors. Serve tossed with spaghetti instead of penne.

MAKES 4 MAIN-COURSE OR 6 FIRST-COURSE SERVINGS

¼ cup (2 fl oz/60 ml) extra-virgin olive oil, plus extra for drizzling

4 cloves garlic, thinly sliced

Generous pinch of red pepper flakes

1 can (35 oz/1.1 kg) plum (Roma) tomatoes, chopped, with juice

Salt

1 lb (500 g) penne

12 fresh basil leaves, coarsely chopped

Leaves from 2 or 3 large fresh marjoram or oregano sprigs, minced

ADDING HEAT

Arrabbiata means "angry" in Italian, and it refers to the use of hot pepper in this variation on a classic marinara sauce. Chiles are not used with the same intensity or creativity in Italian cooking as they are in Mexican or Indian cooking, and fewer varieties were traditionally available. Instead of red pepper flakes, fresh jalapeño chiles can be substituted because their flavor is fairly neutral. Fresh chiles such as poblano, habanero, and serrano, however, would lend a distinctly un-Italian taste to this pasta.

GREEN FARFALLE
WITH GORGONZOLA SAUCE

3 tablespoons unsalted
butter

3 shallots, minced

1 lb (500 g) green or
regular farfalle, fusilli, or
penne

½ cup (4 fl oz/125 ml)
chicken stock

½ lb (250 g) Gorgonzola
dolcelatte cheese, rind
removed, cut into small
pieces

¾ cup (6 fl oz/180 ml)
heavy (double) cream

Grated zest of 1 lemon

Salt and freshly ground
pepper

6 fresh sage leaves,
coarsely chopped

Handful of fresh flat-leaf
(Italian) parsley, coarsely
chopped

Bring a large pot of water to a boil. Meanwhile, in a large frying pan over medium heat, melt the butter. Add the shallots and sauté until soft, about 4 minutes.

Generously salt the boiling water, add the pasta, and cook until al dente, 9–11 minutes.

Reduce the heat under the frying pan to low and add the stock, cheese, cream, and lemon zest. Season with salt and pepper to taste and stir until all the ingredients are smooth and melted, about 4 minutes.

Drain the pasta and add it to the frying pan. Remove from the heat, add the sage and parsley, and toss briefly until the pasta is well coated with the sauce. If the sauce seems too thick, add a bit more chicken stock or a splash of hot water. Pour into a warmed large, shallow bowl. Serve immediately.

MAKES 4 MAIN-COURSE OR 6 FIRST-COURSE SERVINGS

GORGONZOLA STYLES
Italy's famous blue cheese, Gorgonzola is made from cow's milk. When young, it is creamy, soft, and mildly pungent. This version is usually labeled Gorgonzola "dolcelatte" or "dolce." Older, riper Gorgonzola, sometimes labeled "naturale," has a much more pronounced flavor and is a wonderful eating cheese, but it is too strong for this recipe.

LINGUINE WITH ITALIAN TUNA
AND CHERRY TOMATOES

Preheat the oven to 450°F (230°C). Bring a large pot of water to a boil over high heat.

Meanwhile, place the cherry tomatoes on a large rimmed baking sheet. Sprinkle with the green onions and garlic and drizzle with the ¼ cup olive oil. Season with salt and pepper to taste and stir to distribute the seasoning. Bake until the tomatoes turn golden brown at the edges, about 15 minutes.

Generously salt the boiling water, add the linguine, and cook until al dente, 7–9 minutes.

Put the sun-dried tomatoes, tuna, capers, and parsley in a warmed large, shallow bowl. Drain the linguine, add it to the bowl, and drizzle with olive oil. Toss. Add the cherry tomato mixture and toss again gently. Serve immediately.

MAKES 4 MAIN-COURSE OR 6 FIRST-COURSE SERVINGS

2 pints (1½ lb/750 g) cherry tomatoes, stemmed and halved

8 green (spring) onions, including tender green parts, thinly sliced

3 cloves garlic, thinly sliced

¼ cup (2 fl oz/60 ml) extra-virgin olive oil, plus extra for drizzling

Salt and freshly ground pepper

1 lb (500 g) linguine

About 6 oil-packed sun-dried tomatoes, drained and thinly sliced

2 cans (6 oz/185 g each) oil-packed Italian tuna, drained and crumbled

¼ cup (2 oz/60 g) capers, preferably salt packed, soaked and drained (page 50)

Large handful of fresh flat-leaf (Italian) parsley leaves, coarsely chopped

PENNE ALLA VODKA

5 large tomatoes

⅓ cup (3 fl oz/80 ml) extra-virgin olive oil

2 cloves garlic, very thinly sliced

¼ cup (2 fl oz/60 ml) vodka

Salt and freshly ground black pepper

Pinch of red pepper flakes

1 lb (500 g) penne

½ cup (4 fl oz/125 ml) heavy (double) cream

Leaves from 3 or 4 large fresh flat-leaf (Italian) parsley sprigs, coarsely chopped

Bring a large pot of water to a boil. Meanwhile, peel and seed the tomatoes (page 93), then cut them into small dice. If the tomatoes are very juicy, drain them for about 10 minutes in a colander. Set aside.

In a large frying pan over medium heat, warm the olive oil. Add the garlic and sauté until just starting to turn golden, 1–2 minutes. Remove the pan from the heat, add the vodka, return to the heat, and cook until reduced by half. Add the tomatoes, salt and black pepper to taste, and the red pepper flakes and let simmer, uncovered, for 10 minutes.

Generously salt the boiling water, add the pasta, and cook until al dente, 10–12 minutes. Drain well and add the pasta to the frying pan.

Add the cream and stir over medium heat until the penne is well coated with the sauce, about 2 minutes. Taste and adjust the seasoning. Pour into a warmed large, shallow bowl. Add the parsley and toss briefly. Serve immediately.

MAKES 4 MAIN-COURSE OR 6 FIRST-COURSE SERVINGS

COOKING WITH SPIRITS

Vodka may seem like an odd ingredient for an Italian dish, but this Florentine pasta has become a modern classic. When cooking with a strong liquor such as vodka or brandy, it is important to remove the pan from the heat as you add the spirits, and to keep a pan lid ready in case the contents flame up. Add spirits early on in the cooking so that most of the alcohol and its harsh taste can evaporate, leaving behind only the flavor of the liquor.

GEMELLI WITH BROCCOLI, ANCHOVIES, AND SPICY BREAD CRUMBS

ANCHOVY FILLETS

For the most authentic flavor in this dish, use whole salt-packed anchovies that you fillet yourself, available at Italian markets and specialty-food stores. All you need to do is rinse them under cool water to remove excess salt, then run a small knife along the spine to open up the back. Pull off a fillet. Gently lift out the spine, leaving the other fillet free of bones. Taste the anchovy and, if it is very salty, soak it in cool water for several minutes before using.

To make the bread crumbs, in a small frying pan over medium heat, warm the 3 tablespoons olive oil. Add the crumbs, chile, salt to taste, and marjoram and sauté, stirring often, until the bread crumbs are very lightly golden, about 4 minutes. Set aside.

Cut the broccoli into small florets and thinly slice the tender parts of the stems. In a large pot of salted boiling water, blanch the broccoli, cooking for 2 minutes. Scoop the broccoli from the pot with a skimmer, reserving the cooking water, and place in a colander. Rinse under cold water to stop the cooking and to preserve the green color. Let drain.

Return the broccoli-cooking water to a boil, add the pasta, and cook until al dente, 10–12 minutes.

Meanwhile, in a large frying pan over medium heat, warm the ½ cup olive oil. Add the garlic and anchovies and sauté until the garlic is lightly golden, 1–2 minutes. Add the broccoli, red pepper flakes, and salt to taste and sauté for 2–3 minutes. Add the white wine and let it boil away to almost nothing, 1–2 minutes.

Drain the pasta, reserving about ½ cup (4 fl oz/125 ml) of the pasta-cooking water, and add the pasta to the pan. Toss quickly over medium heat to mix well. Add the reserved pasta water as needed to loosen the sauce. Taste and adjust the seasoning.

Pour the pasta into a warmed large, shallow bowl and sprinkle with about half the bread crumbs. Pass the remaining bread crumbs at the table.

MAKES 4 MAIN-COURSE OR 6 FIRST-COURSE SERVINGS

FOR THE BREAD CRUMBS:

3 tablespoons extra-virgin olive oil

¾ cup (1½ oz/45 g) coarse fresh bread crumbs made from day-old coarse country bread

1 jalapeño chile, seeded and finely diced, or generous pinch of red pepper flakes

Salt

Leaves from 2 or 3 large fresh marjoram or oregano sprigs, minced

1 large bunch broccoli (about 1½ lb/750 g)

1 lb (500 g) gemelli, penne, or rigatoni

½ cup (4 fl oz/125 ml) extra-virgin olive oil

5 cloves garlic, thinly sliced

6 anchovy fillets, finely chopped *(far left)*

Pinch of red pepper flakes

Salt

¼ cup (2 fl oz/60 ml) dry white wine

RIGATONI WITH SALAMI, MOZZARELLA, AND ARUGULA

¼ cup (2 fl oz/60 ml) extra-virgin olive oil, plus extra for drizzling

4 cloves garlic, thinly sliced

About 14 plum (Roma) tomatoes, cut into medium dice, or 1 can (35 oz/1.1 kg) plum (Roma) tomatoes, well drained and coarsely chopped

Splash of dry white wine

1 lb (500 g) rigatoni

¼-lb (125-g) chunk salami, cut into small cubes

Salt and freshly ground pepper

½ lb (250 g) mozzarella cheese, cut into small cubes

1 bunch arugula (rocket), stems removed

1 cup (4 oz/125 g) grated pecorino toscano or pecorino romano cheese

Bring a large pot of water to a boil. Meanwhile, in a large frying pan over medium-low heat, warm the ¼ cup olive oil. Add the garlic and sauté it until it is very lightly golden, 1–2 minutes. Add the tomatoes, increase the heat to medium, and cook until the tomatoes begin to release their liquid, 4–5 minutes. Add the white wine and let it boil away for a few minutes.

Generously salt the boiling water, add the pasta, and cook until al dente, 12–14 minutes.

Add the salami to the tomato mixture and season with salt and pepper to taste. Remove from the heat.

Drain the pasta well and put it in a warmed large, shallow bowl. Add the tomato mixture and toss. Add the mozzarella, arugula, and a generous drizzle of olive oil and toss again gently. Add a handful of the grated cheese and toss. Serve immediately. Pass the remaining grated cheese at the table.

MAKES 4 MAIN-COURSE OR 6 FIRST-COURSE SERVINGS

ITALIAN SALAMI

True Italian-made salami is not available to everyone outside of Italy, but many domestic versions are excellent, especially if you buy from a shop that makes its own. For a pasta sauce, try the southern-style *cacciatorini*, *soppressata*, or Genoa-style salami. Many varieties come in a mild or spicy version. Taste-test a piece before cooking with it to make sure you like its flavor. Salami is best in a pasta sauce when cooked only briefly, so add it in the final minutes.

PENNE WITH PROSCIUTTO
AND BUTTER

Bring a large pot of water to a boil. Generously salt the boiling water, add the pasta, and cook until al dente, 10–12 minutes.

Meanwhile, trim the prosciutto of excess fat and cut the slices into narrow strips.

In a large frying pan over medium-low heat, melt the butter. Add the onion and sauté until soft, about 4 minutes. Add the stock and simmer for about 1 minute.

Drain the pasta well and put it in a warmed large, shallow bowl. Add the prosciutto, lemon zest, nutmeg, pepper to taste, chopped parsley, and sage. Pour on the stock mixture and toss well. Add about 3 tablespoons of the cheese and toss again. Garnish with parsley sprigs and serve immediately. Pass the remaining cheese at the table.

MAKES 4 MAIN-COURSE OR 6 FIRST-COURSE SERVINGS

1 lb (500 g) penne

¼ lb (125 g) thinly sliced prosciutto

½ cup (4 oz/125 g) unsalted butter

1 large sweet white onion such as Vidalia, thinly sliced

½ cup (4 fl oz/125 ml) chicken stock

Grated zest of 1 lemon

Generous pinch of freshly grated nutmeg

Freshly ground pepper

Generous handful of fresh flat-leaf (Italian) parsley leaves, coarsely chopped, plus several sprigs

About 5 fresh sage leaves, chopped

1 cup (4 oz/125 g) grated Parmesan cheese

PROSCIUTTO

The famous sweet salt-cured ham from the Parma region, prosciutto di Parma, is now widely available outside of Italy. Other hams can be salty by comparison and less subtle in flavor. When the clerk slices prosciutto for you, make sure it is very thin and the pieces are separated by paper or plastic so that they do not stick together and tear. Prosciutto di San Daniele and prosciutto di Carpegna are two other cured hams from different regions of Italy worth seeking out.

QUICK TOMATO SAUCE
WITH BLACK OLIVES AND CREAM

3 tablespoons unsalted
butter

1 sweet white onion such
as Vidalia, finely diced

1 leek, white part only,
finely diced

4 cloves garlic, thinly
sliced

Tiny splash of brandy or
Cognac

1 can (35 oz/1.1 kg) plum
(Roma) tomatoes, chopped

1 bay leaf

Leaves from 2 or 3 large
fresh thyme sprigs, minced

Salt and freshly ground
pepper

1 lb (500 g) spaghetti or
bucatini

½ cup (2½ oz/75 g) pitted
Mediterranean-style black
olives, halved

½ cup (4 fl oz/125 ml)
heavy (double) cream

Leaves from 3 or 4 large
sprigs flat-leaf (Italian)
parsley, coarsely chopped

1 cup (4 oz/125 g)
grated grana padano or
Parmesan cheese

Bring a large pot of water to a boil. Meanwhile, in a large frying pan over medium heat, melt the butter. Add the onion and leek and sauté until soft, about 5 minutes. Add the garlic and sauté until fragrant and very lightly golden, 1–2 minutes. Add the brandy and let it boil away. Add the tomatoes, bay leaf, and thyme. Raise the heat to high and cook the sauce uncovered, stirring occasionally, until slightly thickened, about 10 minutes. Season with salt and pepper to taste.

Generously salt the boiling water, add the pasta, and cook until al dente, 7–9 minutes.

When the pasta is almost ready, add the olives and cream to the sauce. Simmer gently over low heat for a few minutes to blend the flavors.

Drain the pasta well and add it to the frying pan. Add the parsley and toss gently. Pour into a warmed large, shallow bowl and serve immediately. Pass the cheese at the table.

MAKES 4 MAIN-COURSE OR 6 FIRST-COURSE SERVINGS

GRANA PADANO

A cow's milk grating cheese made in various parts of northern Italy, grana padano is similar to the better-known, richer Parmesan, but it is not aged as long as true Parmesan and as a result has a less complex taste. When bought fresh and freshly grated, grana padano has a wonderful nutty sweetness perfect for many pasta dishes, and it will not overpower delicate sauces the way a longer-aged cheese might.

ELEGANT ENTERTAINING

For special occasions, treat your guests to the kind of dish that they don't eat every day—perhaps one featuring more luxurious ingredients than usual, or a more elaborate presentation. For a formal touch, bring these pastas to the table in individual dishes, rather than serving them family-style in one large bowl.

CRAB RAVIOLI
WITH CRÈME FRAÎCHE AND BASIL
46

CRESPELLE WITH ASPARAGUS AND PORCINI
49

ANGEL HAIR PASTA
WITH SCALLOPS AND ARUGULA
50

SAFFRON TAGLIATELLE
WITH VEAL SAUCE
53

LASAGNE WITH DUCK
AND CHIANTI WINE SAUCE
54

LOBSTER WITH MOSCATO WINE
AND PAPPARDELLE
57

CRAB RAVIOLI
WITH CRÈME FRAÎCHE AND BASIL

CRÈME FRAÎCHE
Crème fraîche tastes something like sour cream, but with a more subtle and interesting flavor. French and domestic brands are widely available, but it is easy to make at home: Combine 1 cup (8 fl oz/250 ml) nonultrapasteurized heavy (double) cream with 1 tablespoon buttermilk in a small saucepan and gently heat to lukewarm. Cover and let sit at room temperature until thickened to the consistency of yogurt, 8–48 hours. The longer it sits, the thicker and tangier it will become. Refrigerate for 3–4 hours to chill before using.

In a large frying pan over medium heat, warm 3 tablespoons of the olive oil. Add half of the green onions and sauté until softened, 3–4 minutes. Add half of the garlic and sauté for 1 minute. Add the crabmeat and cook until just heated through, about 1 minute. Add salt and black pepper to taste, two-thirds of the lemon zest and all of the juice, and the cayenne. Transfer to a bowl. Add the ricotta, the ¼ cup crème fraîche, and the chopped basil. Taste and adjust the seasoning. Mix well, cover, and refrigerate for at least 1 hour or up to 24 hours.

Using the pasta sheets and the crab mixture, prepare the ravioli (page 110) and lay them out on floured baking sheets.

Bring a large pot of water to a boil. Meanwhile, in a large frying pan over medium heat, melt the butter with the remaining 2 tablespoons olive oil. Add the remaining green onions and sauté until they begin to soften, 3–4 minutes. Add the remaining garlic and sauté for 1 minute, not letting it color. Add the tomatoes and salt and black pepper to taste, and cook just until the tomatoes begin to release their juice, about 5 minutes. Add the white wine and boil for 1 minute. Reduce the heat to low, add the 1 tablespoon crème fraîche and the remaining lemon zest, and cook the sauce for 1 minute. Taste and adjust the seasoning.

Generously salt the boiling water, add the ravioli, and cook until tender, 30 seconds–3 minutes, depending on the freshness of the pasta (unless you have a huge pot, you will probably need to do this in 2 batches). Using a skimmer, transfer to paper towels to drain briefly. Put the ravioli in a warmed large, shallow bowl. Pour the sauce over the ravioli and scatter shredded basil on top. Serve immediately.

MAKES 4 MAIN-COURSE OR 6 FIRST-COURSE SERVINGS

5 tablespoons (2½ fl oz/ 75 ml) extra-virgin olive oil

7 green (spring) onions, including tender green parts, thinly sliced

2 cloves garlic, minced

1 lb (500 g) fresh lump crabmeat, picked over for shell fragments

Salt and freshly ground pepper

Grated zest and juice of 1 large lemon

Pinch of cayenne pepper

½ cup (4 oz/125 g) ricotta cheese

¼ cup (2 oz/60 g) plus 1 tablespoon crème fraîche

10 fresh basil leaves, finely chopped, plus fine shreds for garnish

1 lb (500 g) fresh pasta sheets (pages 107–8)

1 tablespoon unsalted butter

4 large tomatoes, peeled and seeded (page 93), then finely diced

Splash of dry white wine

CRESPELLE WITH ASPARAGUS AND PORCINI

Extra-virgin olive oil for drizzling, plus 3 tablespoons

Crespelle Batter *(far right)*

2 lb (1 kg) thick asparagus spears

Salt and freshly ground pepper

Grated zest of 1 lemon

3 cloves garlic, thinly sliced

½ lb (250 g) fresh porcino or shiitake mushrooms, thinly sliced

¼ cup (2 fl oz/60 ml) dry vermouth

1½ cups (12 oz/375 g) ricotta cheese

Large pinch of freshly grated nutmeg

Large handful of fresh flat-leaf (Italian) parsley leaves, coarsely chopped

1 cup (4 oz/125 g) grated Parmesan cheese

1 cup (8 fl oz/250 ml) heavy (double) cream

1 tablespoon truffle oil

Place a 6-inch (15-cm) crepe pan over medium heat and heat a drizzle of olive oil, swirling it to coat the pan. Add 2½–3 tablespoons crespelle batter. Cook until starting to brown at the edges, 30 seconds. Turn with a wooden spatula and cook on the other side for 30 seconds longer. Repeat with the remaining batter, stacking the crespelle on a large plate, until you have 12–15 in all.

Preheat the oven to 425°F (220°C). Trim off the tough ends from the asparagus spears. Using a vegetable peeler and starting about 2 inches (5 cm) below the tip, peel off the thin outer skin from each spear. Put the asparagus on a baking sheet. Drizzle with olive oil and sprinkle with salt and pepper to taste and lemon zest. Place in the oven and roast until fork tender and lightly browned on the edges, about 15 minutes.

In a frying pan over medium heat, warm the 3 tablespoons olive oil. Add the garlic, mushrooms, and salt and pepper to taste, and sauté until the mushrooms are tender and just starting to give off liquid, about 5 minutes. Add the vermouth and boil until almost evaporated. Put the mushroom mixture in a bowl and add the ricotta, nutmeg, half of the parsley, and 2 tablespoons of the grated cheese. Season with salt and pepper to taste and mix gently.

Lightly oil a 9-by-14-by-2-inch (23-by-35-by-5-cm) baking dish. Spread an even layer of the ricotta mixture over each crepe and place 2 or 3 asparagus spears in the center of each one. Roll loosely and place, seam side down, in the baking dish. Pour the cream over the crespelle and sprinkle with the remaining grated cheese. Place in the oven and bake until bubbling hot and lightly browned, about 15 minutes.

Remove the dish from the oven, drizzle the truffle oil over the top, and scatter on the remaining parsley. Serve hot.

MAKES 4 MAIN-COURSE OR 6 FIRST-COURSE SERVINGS

CRESPELLE BATTER

Italy's version of crepes, crespelle are made from some of the same basic ingredients as pasta—flour, eggs, and salt—but prepared in a very different way. In a food processor, combine 1 cup (5 oz/155 g) all-purpose (plain) flour, 3 eggs, 1½ cups (12 fl oz/375 ml) milk, 3 tablespoons olive oil, pinch of salt, and the grated zest of 1 lemon. Process until smooth. Let sit for about 30 minutes to thicken slightly.

ANGEL HAIR PASTA
WITH SCALLOPS AND ARUGULA

SICILIAN CAPERS

Fine Italian capers come from Pantelleria and Salina, two small Sicilian islands. They are packed in salt and have a sweet, floral fragrance, nothing like sharp-tasting brine-packed varieties. Luckily, Sicilian capers are becoming easier to find. Ask for them at Italian specialty-food stores. They are usually sold in large plastic bags. To prepare salted capers, soak them in cool water for about 15 minutes, changing the water once or twice, to remove excess salt. Give them a final rinse and drain well.

Bring a large pot of water to a boil. Meanwhile, rinse the scallops and dry well with paper towels. Season the scallops with salt and pepper to taste. In a large, heavy frying pan over high heat, warm the olive oil until the oil shimmers. In batches without crowding, add the scallops and sear until nicely browned on the first side, about 2 minutes. Turn and brown the other side, about 1 minute longer. Return all the scallops to the pan, add the lemon zest and thyme, and cook for a moment. Using a slotted spoon, remove the scallops from the pan to a bowl. Reduce the heat to low and add the butter and shallots to the pan. Sauté until softened, about 4 minutes.

Generously salt the boiling water, add the pasta, and cook until al dente, 3–4 minutes.

Meanwhile, add the lemon juice and stock to the frying pan and deglaze the pan, stirring to scrape up the browned bits from the bottom. Simmer until slightly thickened, 3–4 minutes.

Drain the pasta well and add it to the frying pan. Return the scallops and any juices that may have accumulated to the pan. Add the capers and the pine nuts. Toss over low heat to finish cooking the scallops and mix the ingredients, about 1 minute. Taste and adjust the seasoning.

Transfer to a warmed large, shallow bowl, add the arugula leaves, and toss gently. Serve immediately.

MAKES 4 MAIN-COURSE OR 6 FIRST-COURSE SERVINGS

1½ lb (750 g) large sea scallops, side muscle removed

Salt and freshly ground pepper

¼ cup (2 fl oz/60 ml) extra-virgin olive oil

Grated zest of 1 lemon

Leaves from 2 or 3 large fresh thyme sprigs, minced

4 tablespoons (2 oz/60 g) unsalted butter

5 shallots, minced

1 lb (500 g) angel hair pasta

Juice of 1 lemon

1 cup (8 fl oz/250 ml) chicken stock

¼ cup (2 oz/60 g) capers, preferably salt-packed, rinsed and drained (far left)

½ cup (2½ oz/75 g) pine nuts, lightly toasted (page 115)

1 large bunch arugula (rocket), preferably small leaved, stems removed

SAFFRON TAGLIATELLE WITH VEAL SAUCE

2 thin slices pancetta

3 shallots

2 cloves garlic

1 carrot, peeled

1 celery stalk

4 tablespoons (2 oz/60 g) unsalted butter

2 tablespoons olive oil

1½ lb (750 g) boneless veal shoulder

Salt and pepper

½ cup (4 fl oz/125 ml) dry white wine

1½ cups (12 fl oz/375 ml) light meat stock (page 111)

1 large piece lemon zest

Leaves from 3 small rosemary sprigs, chopped

Leaves from 2 or 3 large thyme sprigs, chopped

3 tomatoes, peeled and seeded (page 93), then diced

¼ cup (2 fl oz/60 ml) heavy (double) cream

1 lb (500 g) homemade saffron tagliatelle (pages 107–8)

1 cup (4 oz/125 g) grated Parmesan cheese

Chop the pancetta. Mince the shallots and garlic, and finely dice the carrot and celery. In a Dutch oven or heavy flameproof casserole over medium heat, melt 2 tablespoons of the butter with the olive oil. Add the pancetta and sauté until it begins to crisp. Add the shallots, carrot, and celery and sauté until softened and just turning lightly golden, about 6 minutes. Add the garlic and sauté for 1 minute.

Cut the veal shoulder into ¼-inch (6-mm) cubes. Add the veal to the pot, season with salt and pepper, and sauté until it releases its juices and starts to brown, about 15 minutes. Add the white wine and cook until reduced by half. Add the stock, lemon zest, rosemary, thyme, and tomatoes. Again add salt and pepper to taste and bring to a boil. Reduce the heat to low, cover, and braise at a very low simmer, skimming the fat from the surface of the liquid from time to time, until the meat is very tender and the sauce is slightly thickened, about 1½ hours. Add the cream and simmer, uncovered, 2–3 minutes longer to blend the flavors. Taste and adjust the seasoning.

Meanwhile, bring a large pot of water to a boil. Generously salt the boiling water, add the tagliatelle, and cook until tender, 30 seconds–3 minutes, depending on the freshness of the pasta. Drain the pasta well and put it in a warmed large, shallow bowl. Add the remaining 2 tablespoons butter and toss until the butter melts. Add the veal mixture and toss gently. Serve immediately. Pass the grated cheese at the table.

Serving Tip: Garnish with gremolata (right), if desired. Toss the gremolata with the pasta just before serving. The heat from the pasta will release the oils from the gremolata, distributing its flavor.

MAKES 4 MAIN-COURSE OR 6 FIRST-COURSE SERVINGS

GREMOLATA

A mix of finely chopped garlic, lemon zest, and parsley or sometimes sage, gremolata is traditionally sprinkled over osso buco (braised veal shank) as a last-minute embellishment. It is also a wonderful flavoring for this veal sauce. To make gremolata, in a small bowl, mix together the grated zest of 1 lemon; 2 small cloves garlic, minced; and the minced leaves from 5 or 6 large fresh flat-leaf (Italian) parsley sprigs.

LASAGNE WITH DUCK AND CHIANTI WINE SAUCE

BÉCHAMEL SAUCE

To make béchamel sauce, melt
4 tablespoons (2 oz/60 g)
unsalted butter over medium-
low heat. Add 3 tablespoons
all-purpose (plain) flour,
whisking to blend well. Cook,
stirring, for 1–2 minutes. Whisk
in 2 cups (16 fl oz/500 ml)
whole milk. Add 1 bay leaf,
1 clove, and a pinch of allspice
and season with salt to taste.
Bring to a boil, constantly
whisking. Reduce the heat and
simmer, whisking constantly,
until thickened, 4–5 minutes.

In a Dutch oven over medium heat, warm the oil. Brown the duck legs. Remove from the pot and drain off all but 3 tablespoons of fat. Add the leeks and carrot and sauté until softened, about 8 minutes. Add the garlic and sauté it for 1 minute. Add the prosciutto, spices, and half of the herbs. Sauté for 1 minute. Return the duck to the pot. Add the wine, raise the heat to high, and cook to reduce the liquid by half. Add the stock, tomatoes, and salt and pepper to taste. Bring to a boil. Reduce the heat to low, cover, and simmer for 1 hour. Uncover and simmer until the duck is quite tender, about 30 minutes. Skim the excess fat from the surface.

Meanwhile, cook the lasagne sheets in batches in a large pot of salted boiling water until tender, 1–3 minutes. Lay them on damp kitchen towels until ready to assemble the lasagne.

Remove the duck legs from the pot, discard the skin and bones, and cut the meat into small pieces. Return the meat to the pot. Simmer, partially covered, until the sauce is quite thick, 15 minutes. Add the rest of the herbs. Taste and adjust the seasoning.

Preheat the oven to 425°F (220°C). Lightly oil a 10-by-12-inch (25-by-30-cm) baking dish or equivalent. Add a layer of lasagne sheets, cutting to fit as necessary, and top with one-third of the duck sauce. Sprinkle with ½ cup (2 oz/60 g) of the cheese. Repeat with two more layers of lasagne, duck sauce, and cheese, then end with a layer of lasagne. Remove the bay leaf and clove from the béchamel, and pour over the lasagne, letting the béchamel run down the insides of the pan a bit. Sprinkle with the remaining cheese and bake until golden and bubbling hot, about 20 minutes. Let rest for 3–4 minutes before serving.

MAKES 4–6 MAIN-COURSE SERVINGS

3 tablespoons olive oil

4 whole duck legs (with thighs)

4 leeks, white part only, cut into small dice

1 carrot, peeled and cut into small dice

2 cloves garlic, minced

4 thin slices prosciutto, chopped

Pinch of ground cloves

Pinch of ground allspice

Leaves from 3 or 4 small fresh rosemary sprigs, minced

8 fresh sage leaves, minced

1 cup (8 fl oz/250 ml) Chianti or other dry red wine

1 cup (8 fl oz/250 ml) chicken stock

1 can (35 oz/1.1 kg) plum (Roma) tomatoes, drained and chopped

Salt and pepper

1 lb (500 g) lasagne sheets (pages 107–8) or purchased fresh pasta sheets

2 cups (8 oz/250 g) grated Parmesan cheese

Béchamel Sauce for topping lasagne (far left)

LOBSTER WITH MOSCATO WINE AND PAPPARDELLE

2 live lobsters, about 1½ lb (750 g) each

Salt and freshly ground pepper

4 tablespoons (2 oz/60 g) unsalted butter

5 tablespoons (2½ fl oz/ 75 ml) extra-virgin olive oil

½ cup (4 fl oz/125 ml) Moscato or other sweet dessert wine

½ cup (4 fl oz/125 ml) chicken stock

5 shallots, very thinly sliced

4 large tomatoes, peeled and seeded (page 93), then diced

1 lb (500 g) fresh pappardelle, homemade (pages 107–8) or purchased

½ cup (2½ oz/75 g) pine nuts, lightly toasted (page 115)

12 fresh basil leaves, cut into thin strips, plus several large sprigs

Put the lobsters in a large pot of salted boiling water, cover, and cook for 4–5 minutes. The lobster meat will pull away from the shells, but be slightly undercooked in the center. Remove the lobsters from the pot, reserving the cooking water, put the lobsters in a shallow pan, and let cool slightly. Remove all the meat *(right)*, catching any juices in the pan and reserving the meat and shells.

In a large saucepan over medium heat, melt 1 tablespoon of the butter with 1 tablespoon of the olive oil. Add the lobster shells and sauté for 3–4 minutes. Add the wine and cook until reduced by half. Add the stock and simmer for about 5 minutes. Add any juices reserved from shelling the lobster. Strain the broth through a fine-mesh sieve into a bowl and discard the shells.

In a large frying pan over medium heat, melt the remaining 3 tablespoons butter. Add the shallots and sauté until soft, about 4 minutes. Add the tomatoes and sauté for 1 minute. Add the lobster broth and simmer for another 5 minutes or until the sauce is reduced slightly. Add salt and pepper to taste.

Return the lobster-cooking water to a boil, add the pasta, and cook until tender, 30 seconds–3 minutes, depending on the freshness of the pasta.

Meanwhile, chop the lobster meat into small chunks and add it to the frying pan. Simmer over low heat for 1 minute; do not overcook. Taste again and adjust the seasoning.

Drain the pasta and put it in a warmed large, shallow bowl. Drizzle with the remaining 4 tablespoons (2 fl oz/60 ml) olive oil and toss gently. Add the lobster mixture, pine nuts, and basil strips and toss again. Garnish with basil sprigs and serve immediately.

MAKES 4 MAIN-COURSE OR 6 FIRST-COURSE SERVINGS

CRACKING LOBSTER

To remove the meat of a cooked lobster, first twist off the lobster's claws, crack the claws with a lobster cracker or mallet, and pry out the meat with a fork. Slice the lobster body in half lengthwise, starting where the tail and body intersect and cutting first through the tail and then through the rest of the body and head. Remove and discard the black vein and the small sac at the base of the head. Remove the meat from the body. Grasp the tail and pry out the meat with the fork.

SPRING AND SUMMER

As winter fades, home cooks delight at new vegetables coming into season. Asparagus, artichokes, and tender beans appear in early spring, creating light but substantial pasta dishes. Before long, ripe tomatoes and vibrantly colored bell peppers (capsicums) herald the peak of summer and go into luscious sauces.

LASAGNETTE WITH ASPARAGUS AND MORELS

MOREL MUSHROOMS

Fresh morel mushrooms are a springtime delicacy. Their earthy perfume marries well with that of spring vegetables, especially asparagus. When buying morels, look for ones that have a fresh mushroom smell and feel heavy. Turn down any that look shriveled or, worse, mushy and water-logged. To clean morels' many crevices, swish them briefly in a bowl of water. Other flavorful mushrooms such as chanterelles, shiitakes, or portobellos can be substituted.

Trim off the tough stem ends from the asparagus spears. Using a vegetable peeler and starting about 2 inches (5 cm) below the tip, peel off the thin outer skin from each spear. Cut on the diagonal into ½-inch (12-mm) pieces. Plunge the asparagus into a large pot of salted boiling water and blanch for 1 minute. Using a large skimmer, transfer the asparagus to a colander, reserving the cooking water. Run cold water over the asparagus to preserve its bright green color and to stop the cooking. Drain the asparagus and set aside.

In a large frying pan over medium heat, warm the ⅓ cup olive oil. Add the onion and sauté until soft and just starting to turn golden, about 5 minutes. Add the garlic, morels, asparagus, and salt and pepper to taste and sauté for 2 minutes. Pour in the stock and simmer until the vegetables are tender, 4–5 minutes. Add the thyme and lemon juice and mix well.

While the vegetables are simmering, return the reserved asparagus-cooking water to a boil. Add the pasta and cook until al dente, 7–9 minutes. Drain well and add to the frying pan. Add the pine nuts and parsley and toss briefly to blend all the ingredients. Taste and adjust the seasoning, adding a drizzle of olive oil.

Transfer the pasta to a warmed large, shallow bowl and sprinkle about 3 tablespoons of the cheese over the top. Pass the remaining cheese at the table.

MAKES 4 MAIN-COURSE OR 6 FIRST-COURSE SERVINGS

2 lb (1 kg) thick asparagus spears

Salt and freshly ground pepper

⅓ cup (3 fl oz/80 ml) extra-virgin olive oil, plus extra for drizzling

1 large, sweet white onion such as Vidalia, diced

3 cloves garlic, minced

½ lb (250 g) fresh morel mushrooms, quartered

½ cup (4 fl oz/125 ml) chicken or vegetable stock

Leaves from 5 large fresh thyme sprigs, coarsely chopped

Juice of 1 lemon

1 lb (500 g) lasagnette or spaghetti

½ cup pine nuts (2½ oz/ 75 g), lightly toasted (page 115)

Handful of fresh flat-leaf (Italian) parsley leaves, coarsely chopped

1 cup (4 oz/125 g) grated pecorino toscano or pecorino romano cheese

PASTA SALAD WITH BABY ARTICHOKES AND GRILLED TUNA

1 lb (500 g) cavatappi, penne, ziti, or fusilli

Salt and freshly ground pepper

10 tablespoons (5 fl oz/ 160 ml) extra-virgin olive oil

About 20 baby artichokes, trimmed and halved lengthwise *(far right)*

3 cloves garlic, very thinly sliced

½ cup (4 fl oz/125 ml) dry white wine

½ cup (4 fl oz/125 ml) warm water

3 ripe tomatoes, peeled and seeded (page 93), then diced

1 lb (500 g) tuna steak, 1½ inches (4 cm) thick

½ red onion, thinly sliced

Grated zest and juice of 1 large orange

Leaves from 5 or 6 large fresh mint sprigs, coarsely chopped

Leaves from 5 or 6 large fresh marjoram sprigs, coarsely chopped

Bring a large pot of water to a boil. Generously salt the boiling water, add the pasta, and cook until al dente, 8–11 minutes. Drain and rinse briefly under cold water to stop the cooking and remove excess starch. (This step is only for pasta to be served in a salad.) Drain well and put in a large bowl. Toss with 3 tablespoons of the olive oil (to prevent sticking) and set aside at room temperature.

In a frying pan over medium heat, warm 3 tablespoons of the olive oil. Drain the artichokes well and add them, along with the garlic, to the pan. Season with salt and pepper to taste. Sauté until the artichokes are just turning golden at the edges, about 5 minutes. Add the white wine and let it boil away. Add the water, reduce the heat to medium-low, and simmer, uncovered, until the artichokes are tender, about 5 minutes. (If the liquid evaporates before the artichokes are tender, add a little extra warm water.) Remove from the heat, add the tomatoes, and toss gently.

Preheat a broiler (grill), or heat a grill pan over high heat. Coat the tuna lightly with olive oil and season with salt and pepper to taste. Sear the tuna on one side without moving it until the bottom edges are nicely browned, 4–5 minutes. Turn and sear the other side until the fish just starts to flake when prodded with a fork, about 4 minutes. The center should be slightly pink. Let cool and cut into small chunks, discarding any bones.

Add the artichoke mixture, onion, orange zest and juice, and herbs to the pasta. Add the tuna, the remaining olive oil, and a bit more salt and pepper. Toss gently. Taste and adjust the seasoning. This salad is best served right away, but it can sit at room temperature for up to 2 hours.

MAKES 4 MAIN-COURSE OR 6 FIRST-COURSE SERVINGS

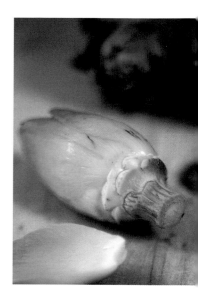

BABY ARTICHOKES
Baby artichokes are not immature artichokes, but rather smaller ones that grow lower down on the stalk. They do not have chokes and so are simpler to prepare than the large ones. To ready them for this recipe, starting at the base of each artichoke, pull off and discard the tough outer leaves. Cut the stem off flush with the base and halve the artichoke. As they are trimmed, drop them into a bowl of water mixed with the juice of 1 lemon to minimize discoloration.

TAGLIATELLE WITH FAVA BEANS, MASCARPONE, AND PROSCIUTTO

Bring a large pot of water to a boil. Meanwhile, in a large frying pan over medium heat, melt the butter with the olive oil. Add the leeks and sauté until soft, 5–6 minutes. Add the fava beans, salt and pepper to taste, and nutmeg and sauté for 1 minute. Add the stock and simmer until the beans are just tender to the bite, about 4 minutes.

Generously salt the boiling water, add the pasta, and cook until tender, 1–3 minutes, depending on the freshness of the pasta.

Remove the frying pan from the heat and add the mascarpone and lemon zest, stirring until the cheese is melted. (High heat can make mascarpone separate.)

Drain and pour the pasta into a warmed large, shallow bowl. Add the fava bean mixture and toss briefly. Add the prosciutto, basil, and about 2 tablespoons of the grated cheese. Toss. Taste and season with salt and pepper. (Depending on the saltiness of the prosciutto, you may not need extra salt.) Serve immediately. Pass the remaining cheese at the table.

MAKES 4 MAIN-COURSE OR 6 FIRST-COURSE SERVINGS

SKINNING FAVA BEANS

Fava beans are delicious, but they require a bit of work. They must first be removed from their long, green pods, and each individual bean is covered with a tough skin that must be removed before cooking (unless the beans are very young and fresh). To peel, plunge the beans into boiling water and blanch for about 1 minute. Drain and rinse under cool water. The skins should slip off easily when the beans are pinched between the thumb and fore-finger; use a paring knife to help remove stubborn ones.

3 tablespoons unsalted butter

3 tablespoons olive oil

5 leeks, white part only, cut into thin rounds

3 lb (1.5 kg) fava (broad) beans, shelled and skinned (far left)

Salt and freshly ground pepper

3 or 4 gratings nutmeg

1 cup (8 fl oz/250 ml) chicken stock (page 111)

1 lb (500 g) homemade tagliatelle (pages 107–8) or purchased fresh fettuccine

½ cup (4 oz/125 g) mascarpone cheese, at room temperature

Grated zest of 1 large lemon

¼ lb (125 g) thin-sliced prosciutto, trimmed of excess fat and cut into narrow strips

Generous handful of fresh basil leaves, finely shredded

½ cup (2 oz/60 g) grated grana padano or Parmesan cheese

SPAGHETTI WITH ZUCCHINI BLOSSOMS AND SAFFRON

¼ cup (2 fl oz/60 ml) olive oil

1 large sweet white onion such as Vidalia, thinly sliced

1½ lb (750 g) small zucchini (courgettes), cut into rounds

Salt and freshly ground pepper

1 lb (500 g) spaghetti

Generous pinch of saffron threads, toasted and ground (page 90)

¾ cup (6 fl oz/180 ml) chicken or vegetable stock, heated

Grated zest of 1 lemon

Leaves from 3 or 4 large fresh thyme sprigs, chopped

About 12 zucchini (courgette) blossoms, trimmed and halved lengthwise

3 tablespoons unsalted butter

1 cup (4 oz/125 g) grated grana padano or Parmesan cheese

Bring a large pot of water to a boil. Meanwhile, in a large frying pan over medium-high heat, warm the olive oil. Add the onion, sliced zucchini, and salt and pepper to taste, and sauté until the vegetables are tender and golden at the edges, 7–8 minutes.

Generously salt the boiling water, add the spaghetti, and cook until al dente, 7–9 minutes.

Meanwhile, dissolve the saffron in the hot stock. Add the saffron mixture, lemon zest, and thyme to the frying pan and simmer on low heat for 2–3 minutes to blend the flavors. Add the zucchini blossoms and heat through until wilted, about 1 minute.

Drain the pasta and put it in a warmed large, shallow bowl. Add the butter and 2 heaping tablespoons of the grated cheese. Toss. Add the sauce and toss gently. Serve immediately. Pass the remaining cheese at the table.

MAKES 4 MAIN-COURSE OR 6 FIRST-COURSE SERVINGS

ZUCCHINI BLOSSOMS
You'll find zucchini blossoms at farmers' markets and in some grocery stores starting in early June and through the middle of the summer. They are best when first picked and fully open, so try to use them the day you buy them. You can prolong their freshness for a day or so by sticking their stems in water and refrigerating them. Gently wash the blossoms in cool water to remove any dirt or little bugs, and pinch off the stamen. Dry the blossoms on paper towels.

COUSCOUS WITH MUSSELS, TOMATOES, AND TARRAGON BUTTER

PREPARING MUSSELS

Cultivated mussels are what you find now in most fish markets. They have good flavor and are almost dirt free, so cleaning—which is such a chore with wild mussels—is reduced to a quick rinse under cold water. The beard, weedy fibers that extend from between the shells, is usually minimal in the cultivated variety, but if you buy locally harvested wild mussels, you'll have to pull the beard off each one just before cooking.

Put the butter in a small bowl and mix in the chopped tarragon and the garlic. Season with salt and pepper to taste. Cover and refrigerate the tarragon butter if not using right away. (This can be made a day or two ahead, if desired.)

In a saucepan over high heat, bring the stock to a boil. Reduce the heat to low, add half of the coriander and fennel, the honey, and the bay leaf and simmer for 2–3 minutes. Remove from the heat, add half of the tarragon butter, and stir until melted. Add salt if needed. Put the couscous in a large, shallow bowl, pour in the hot stock mixture, and mix briefly. Cover with aluminum foil.

Peel and seed the tomatoes (page 93), then dice them. Set aside.

In a pot large enough to hold all the mussels when opened, warm the olive oil over medium heat. Add the green onions and the remaining coriander and fennel. Sauté until the green onions just start to soften and the spices are fragrant, about 2 minutes. Add the mussels (discarding any that do not close to the touch), tomatoes, and a generous splash of liqueur, and cook, stirring occasionally, until the mussels open, about 1 minute. Discard any that do not open. Remove from the heat, add the remaining tarragon butter and the parsley, and stir until the butter is melted.

Uncover the couscous and fluff it with a fork. The grains should now be tender and all the stock absorbed. Spoon the couscous into a serving bowl, top it with with the mussels and their broth, and garnish the dish with tarragon sprigs before serving.

MAKES 4 MAIN-COURSE OR 6 FIRST-COURSE SERVINGS

5 tablespoons (2½ oz/75 g) unsalted butter, at room temperature

Leaves from 6 or 7 fresh tarragon sprigs, chopped, plus several sprigs

2 cloves garlic, minced

Salt and freshly ground pepper

2½ cups (20 fl oz/625 ml) chicken stock

1 tablespoon ground coriander

1 tablespoon ground fennel

1 tablespoon honey

1 bay leaf

2 cups (12 oz/375 g) instant couscous

3 large tomatoes

3 tablespoons olive oil

10 green (spring) onions, including tender green parts, thinly sliced

3 lb (1.5 kg) mussels, scrubbed and debearded

Splash of anise liqueur

Large handful of fresh flat-leaf (Italian) parsley leaves, coarsely chopped

BUCATINI WITH SHRIMP SKEWERS AND SICILIAN PESTO

FOR THE SICILIAN PESTO:

½ cup (3 oz/90 g) blanched almonds

2 cloves garlic

1 green or red peperoncini chile or jalapeño chile, seeded and chopped

½ cup (4 fl oz/125 ml) extra-virgin olive oil

24 fresh basil leaves

Handful of fresh flat-leaf (Italian) parsley leaves

2 or 3 large fresh mint sprigs

2 tomatoes, peeled and seeded (page 93), then diced

Salt

3 tablespoons extra-virgin olive oil

Grated zest and juice of 1 lemon

½ teaspoon ground cumin

Salt and pepper

1½ lb (750 g) large shrimp (prawns)

1 lb (500 g) bucatini, linguine, or spaghetti

To make the pesto, combine the almonds, garlic, chile, and olive oil in a blender or food processor and grind to a coarse paste. Add the basil, parsley, and mint and process until just blended. Do not process to a smooth purée; it should have some texture. Pour into a bowl. Add the tomatoes and salt to taste, and mix until blended.

Bring a large pot of water to a boil. Light a fire in a grill, preheat a broiler (grill), or heat a grill pan over high heat.

Meanwhile, combine the olive oil, lemon zest and juice, cumin, and salt and pepper to taste in a large bowl to make a marinade. Shell the shrimp, leaving the tails intact, and devein them if the vein is visible (page 115). Add the shrimp to the marinade and mix well. Thread the shrimp on 4 long metal skewers for a main course, or 6 shorter skewers for a first course. Brush the shrimp with the oil remaining in the bowl.

Generously salt the boiling water, add the bucatini, and cook until al dente, 10–12 minutes.

Meanwhile, sear the shrimp skewers on the grill or in the broiler without moving them until they start to turn pink, 1–2 minutes. Turn and cook the other side until evenly pink, 1–2 minutes. Do not overcook.

Drain the pasta, reserving about ½ cup (4 fl oz/125 ml) of the pasta-cooking water. Put the pasta in a warmed large, shallow bowl. Pour on the pesto and toss, adding a few tablespoons of the cooking water to loosen the sauce, if necessary. Serve the pasta alongside the shrimp, removing the skewers if desired. Serve immediately.

MAKES 4 MAIN-COURSE OR 6 FIRST-COURSE SERVINGS

SICILIAN PESTO

Unlike the well-known Genoese pesto (page 25), the Sicilian variety contains tomatoes and usually omits cheese, making it a perfect match for seafood (fish and cheese are not usually combined in Italian pasta dishes). Also, almonds replace the pine nuts used in the Genoese version, giving the Sicilian sauce a distinct southern Italian character that reflects an Arabic influence.

PENNE WITH ROASTED PEPPERS AND SWEET VERMOUTH

Preheat the broiler (grill). Place the peppers on a broiler pan and broil, turning them often, until charred on all sides. Slip the peppers into a paper bag and let them steam for a few minutes, then peel off the blackened skin. (Do not rinse the peppers, or you will wash away flavor; a few black specks are acceptable.) Remove the stems and seeds, and cut the peppers into long, narrow strips. Place the strips in a small bowl to save their juices.

Bring a large pot of water to a boil. Meanwhile, in a large frying pan over medium heat, melt the butter with the 3 tablespoons olive oil. Add the green onions and sauté until softened, about 2 minutes. Add the bell pepper strips, pinch of nutmeg, and salt and pepper to taste, and sauté until the peppers are tender and very fragrant, about 5 minutes. Add the vermouth and cook to reduce it by half, about 2 minutes.

Generously salt the boiling water, add the pasta, and cook until al dente, 10–12 minutes. Drain, reserving about ½ cup of the pasta-cooking water. Add the pasta to the frying pan and sauté briefly over low heat to blend the flavors, adding a few table-spoons of cooking water to loosen the sauce, if needed. Transfer to a warmed large, shallow bowl. Add 2 heaping tablespoons of the cheese, the basil strips, and a drizzle of olive oil. Toss. Taste and adjust the seasoning (you may not need extra salt due to the saltiness of the cheese). Garnish with basil sprigs. Serve hot or at room temperature, passing the remaining cheese at the table.

MAKES 4 MAIN-COURSE OR 6 FIRST-COURSE SERVINGS

RICOTTA SALATA
This dried and salted ricotta cheese has a soft but crumbly texture that won't melt into creaminess when tossed with hot pasta. Instead, it will punctuate your sauce with bits of salty tang. Usually, the older the cheese, the saltier. In the spring, look for young ricotta salata in your cheese shop (it is sometimes labeled "spring ricotta salata"); this tends to be less salty and a bit softer.

6 bell peppers (capsicums), preferably a mixture of red, yellow, and orange

2 tablespoons unsalted butter

3 tablespoons extra-virgin olive oil, plus extra for drizzling

About 8 green (spring) onions, including tender green parts, thinly sliced

Freshly grated nutmeg

Salt and freshly ground pepper

½ cup (4 fl oz/125 ml) sweet red vermouth

1 lb (500 g) penne

¼ lb (125 g) ricotta salata or feta cheese, grated or finely crumbled

About 12 fresh basil leaves, cut into narrow strips, plus sprigs for garnish

72

AUTUMN AND WINTER

Rich aromas and deep flavors are the rewards of cold-weather cooking. As autumn days grow shorter, sturdy vegetables, large shaped pastas, canned tomatoes, and meats such as fresh sausage and stewing cuts grow in appeal. In winter, when many fresh vegetables are out of season, hearty dishes may be spiced up with anchovies, olives, capers, and citrus zest from the pantry.

FUSILLI WITH BRAISED FENNEL, SWEET SAUSAGE, AND PECORINO

In a Dutch oven or large, heavy flameproof casserole dish over medium heat, warm 3 tablespoons of the olive oil. Add the leeks, sliced fennel, ground fennel seeds, and salt and pepper to taste and sauté until the vegetables begin to soften, about 5 minutes. Add the wine and cook until reduced by half. Add the chicken stock, cover, and cook until the vegetables are tender, about 10 minutes.

Bring a large pot of water to a boil. Meanwhile, warm the remaining 2 tablespoons olive oil in a heavy frying pan over high heat. Add the sausage, breaking it up with a spoon. Cook until well browned, then season with salt and pepper to taste. Pour off most of the fat (keep a little to add flavor) and add a tiny splash of sherry vinegar.

Generously salt the boiling water, add the pasta, and cook until al dente, 8–11 minutes.

Meanwhile, add the sausage to the pot with the fennel and simmer for 1–2 minutes to blend the flavors. You should have some liquid left in the pot to form a sauce. If not, add a little warm water or more chicken stock. Taste and adjust the seasoning and add a drizzle of olive oil.

Drain the pasta and put it in a warmed large, shallow bowl. Add a drizzle of olive oil, the tarragon and parsley, and about 3 tablespoons of the cheese. Toss. Add the fennel mixture, toss again, and serve immediately. Pass the remaining cheese at the table.

MAKES 4 MAIN-COURSE OR 6 FIRST-COURSE SERVINGS

PECORINO CHEESE
Made from sheep's milk, pecorino is produced in nearly every region of central and southern Italy. Each area's cheese has its own distinct taste. Pecorino romano, made around Rome, tends to be well aged and sharp. Pecorino toscano, from Tuscany, is mild and creamy when young, and stronger and drier when aged. Other famous pecorinos are made in Sicily and Sardinia. Look for these cheeses at well-stocked supermarkets or cheese shops, and taste-test several varieties so you can get to know their characteristics.

5 tablespoons (2½ fl oz/ 75 ml) extra-virgin olive oil, plus extra for drizzling

4 leeks, white part only, thinly sliced

2 fennel bulbs, trimmed, cored, and thinly sliced

½ teaspoon fennel seeds, ground to a powder

Salt and freshly ground pepper

½ cup (4 fl oz/125 ml) dry white wine

¾ cup (6 fl oz/180 ml) chicken stock

1 lb (500 g) sweet Italian pork sausages, casings removed and crumbled

Splash of sherry vinegar

1 lb (500 g) fusilli lunghi or regular fusilli

Leaves from 6 large fresh tarragon sprigs, coarsely chopped

Handful of fresh flat-leaf (Italian) parsley leaves, coarsely chopped

1 cup (4 oz/125 g) grated pecorino toscano or pecorino romano cheese

PENNE WITH BUTTERNUT SQUASH, SAGE, AND BRESAOLA

3 tablespoons extra-virgin olive oil, plus extra for drizzling

5 shallots, minced

1 butternut squash, peeled, seeded, and cut into small dice

Pinch of ground allspice

Salt and freshly ground pepper

¾ cup (6 fl oz/180 ml) chicken stock

Splash of balsamic vinegar

1 lb (500 g) penne

8 fresh sage leaves, cut into narrow strips

¼ lb (125 g) thinly sliced bresaola or prosciutto, cut into narrow strips

1 cup (4 oz/125 g) grated grana padano or Parmesan cheese

Bring a large pot of water to a boil. Meanwhile, in a Dutch oven or flameproof casserole dish over medium heat, warm the 3 tablespoons olive oil. Add the shallots and cook until softened, 3–4 minutes. Add the squash and allspice and season with salt and pepper to taste. Sauté for 1–2 minutes. Add the stock, reduce the heat to medium-low, cover, and simmer until the squash is fork tender, about 8 minutes. (Don't stir the squash while cooking, or it will break down into a purée. You want to keep the pieces whole.) Turn off the heat and add the balsamic vinegar. Taste and adjust the seasoning.

Generously salt the boiling water, add the pasta, and cook until al dente, 10–12 minutes.

Drain the pasta and put it in a warmed large, shallow bowl. Pour on the squash mixture. Add the sage, bresaola, and a drizzle of olive oil and toss gently. Sprinkle with some of the cheese and serve immediately. Pass the remaining cheese at the table.

MAKES 4 MAIN-COURSE OR 6 FIRST-COURSE SERVINGS

BRESAOLA

This salt-cured, air-dried beef fillet is a specialty of the Valtellina, an Alpine valley in Lombardy. It is usually served thinly sliced, like prosciutto, and eaten as an appetizer. Its taste is a little less salty than that of prosciutto, but its texture is firmer. Bresaola is wonderful in a pasta sauce, but add it at the last minute so it doesn't cook much (this will spoil its delicate taste). Prosciutto can be substituted in a pinch.

CANNELLONI WITH GOAT CHEESE AND ROASTED TOMATOES

ROASTED TOMATOES

Quarter about 20 plum (Roma) tomatoes and place them on a large foil-lined baking sheet. Drizzle with 3 tablespoons olive oil and sprinkle with 3 cloves garlic, thinly sliced, and the chopped leaves of 2 small sprigs of thyme. Season with salt and pepper to taste and toss to distribute the seasonings. Roast at 450°F (230°C) until the tomatoes start turning golden brown at the edges, about 20 minutes. Remove from the oven and sprinkle with a handful of chopped fresh flat-leaf (Italian) parsley leaves.

Preheat the oven to 450°F (230°C). Plunge the escarole into a pot of boiling salted water and blanch for 1 minute. Scoop out with a skimmer, reserving the cooking water, and run cold water over the greens to stop the cooking. Squeeze out excess water.

In a large frying pan over medium heat, warm the olive oil. Sauté the shallots until soft, about 4 minutes. Add the garlic and sauté until just golden. Add the escarole, anchovies, and salt and pepper to taste, and sauté just until tender, 2–3 minutes. Drain the raisins and add them along with the pine nuts, a squeeze of lemon juice, and 2 tablespoons of the Parmesan. Mix well.

Meanwhile, bring the escarole-cooking water back to a boil and cook the pasta a few sheets at a time until tender, 1–2 minutes, depending on the freshness of the pasta. Scoop them out with a skimmer and place in a colander. Run cold water over them to cool. Drain and lay them out on damp kitchen towels.

Lightly coat a 9-by-14-by-2-inch (23-by-35-by-5-cm) baking dish with olive oil. Spread an even layer of the escarole over each pasta square, leaving a border of ¼ inch (6 mm). Crumble the goat cheese and scatter it over the escarole. Roll the cannelloni loosely and place, seam side down, in the baking dish. They should fit fairly snugly. Layer the tomatoes evenly over the top. Drizzle with the cream and sprinkle with the remaining Parmesan. Bake until bubbling hot and lightly browned at the edges, about 15 minutes. Serve at once.

MAKES 4 MAIN-COURSE OR 6 FIRST-COURSE SERVINGS

Leaves from 3 heads escarole (Batavian endive), chopped

¼ cup (2 fl oz/60 ml) extra-virgin olive oil

3 shallots, thinly sliced

4 cloves garlic, thinly sliced

4 anchovy fillets, chopped

Salt and freshly ground pepper

½ cup (3 oz/90 g) golden raisins (sultanas), soaked briefly in warm water

½ cup (2½ oz/75 g) pine nuts, lightly toasted (page 115)

Fresh lemon juice

¾ cup (3 oz/90 g) grated Parmesan cheese

1 lb (500 g) fresh pasta cut for cannelloni (pages 107–8)

1 log (11 oz/345 g) fresh goat cheese

About 20 Roasted Tomatoes *(far left)*

¾ cup (6 fl oz/180 ml) heavy (double) cream

PAPPARDELLE WITH CHICKEN, ROSEMARY, AND GREEN OLIVES

3 chicken legs with thighs

Salt and pepper

6 tablespoons (3 fl oz/80 ml) extra-virgin olive oil

2 thin slices pancetta, chopped

1 yellow onion, diced

2 small celery stalks, diced, plus chopped leaves

1 carrot, peeled and diced

2 small whole rosemary sprigs, plus minced leaves from 1 small sprig

1 bay leaf

2 juniper berries, crushed

½ cup (4 fl oz/125 ml) dry vermouth

½ cup (4 fl oz/125 ml) chicken stock

1 can (35 oz/1.1 kg) plum (Roma) tomatoes, chopped

2 chicken livers, membranes snipped and lobes separated

½ cup (2½ oz/75 g) green olives, pitted and halved

1 lb (500 g) fresh pappardelle (pages 107–8) or 1 lb dried pappardelle

Rinse the chicken legs, pat dry, and season them with salt and pepper to taste. In a large Dutch oven or heavy flameproof casserole dish over medium heat, warm 3 tablespoons of the olive oil. When the oil is hot, add the chicken and brown well on all sides. Remove the chicken from the pot. Pour off all but 2 tablespoons of the fat. Add the pancetta to the pot and cook until crisp. Add the onion, celery and leaves, and carrot and sauté until the vegetables are soft and fragrant, about 8 minutes. Add the rosemary sprigs, bay leaf, and juniper berries and sauté for 1 minute. Return the chicken to the pot. Add the vermouth and cook until reduced by half. Add the chicken stock, tomatoes, and a bit more salt. Bring to a boil. Reduce the heat to low, cover, and simmer until the chicken is very tender, about 1¼ hours. Skim the fat from the sauce once or twice during cooking. Remove the chicken pieces and, when cool enough to handle, remove the meat and chop it into small pieces, discarding the bones and skin. Set aside.

Rinse the chicken livers well, pat dry, and season them with salt and pepper to taste. In a small sauté pan over high heat, warm 1 tablespoon of the olive oil. Sauté the chicken livers until well browned on both sides but still a bit pink at the center, about 2 minutes. Chop them into small pieces and add to the sauce along with the chopped chicken. Add the olives and taste for seasoning.

Meanwhile, bring a large pot of water to a boil. Generously salt the boiling water, add the pasta, and cook until al dente, 1–2 minutes for fresh, and 8–10 minutes for dried. Drain well. Put the pasta in a warmed large, shallow bowl. Toss with the remaining 2 tablespoons olive oil and the minced rosemary leaves. Add the chicken mixture and toss again. Serve at once.

MAKES 4 MAIN-COURSE OR 6 FIRST-COURSE SERVINGS

GREEN OLIVES

All olives start out green, turning brown, purple, or black as they mature. Green olives are tart and firm, blending well with other strong flavors, such as the rosemary in this sauce. Try the bright green picholine olives from France or the milder Cerignola from southern Italy. Cracked green Sicilian olives are another good choice. Taste-test any olives you plan to use in a pasta dish. If they are very salty, blanch the batch in boiling water for 1 minute to soften their flavor.

MINESTRONE WITH CABBAGE AND TUBETTI

Pick over the beans, discarding any stones or misshapen beans. Rinse well, place in a bowl, add water to cover by 2 inches (5 cm), and soak for 4–12 hours. Drain and place in a large pot. Add water to cover by about 3 inches (7.5 cm).

Trim the leeks, the fennel, and the carrots, reserving all the trimmings. Peel the carrots. Finely dice all the vegetables and set aside. Add the leek, fennel, and carrot trimmings to the pot with the beans, and season with a pinch of salt and the bay leaf. Bring to a boil, reduce the heat to low, cover, and simmer gently until the beans are tender, about 1 hour.

Bring a large pot of water to a boil. Generously salt the boiling water, add the pasta, and cook until al dente, 8–10 minutes. Drain and toss with 2 tablespoons of the olive oil.

Finely chop the pancetta. In a large pot over medium heat, warm the remaining 3 tablespoons olive oil. Add the pancetta and sauté until crisp, about 4 minutes. Add the diced leeks, fennel, carrots, and salt and pepper to taste and sauté until the vegetables are just starting to soften, about 5 minutes. Add the garlic and sauté until fragrant, about 1 minute. Add the cabbage and rosemary and sauté for about 1 minute. Add the tomatoes and stock and bring to a boil. Remove the vegetable trimmings and bay leaf from the beans and add the beans with their liquid to the pot. Reduce the heat to low and simmer, uncovered, until all the vegetables are very tender, 15–20 minutes. Add the pasta and parsley and heat through. Taste for seasoning. Ladle into soup bowls, drizzle each serving with olive oil, and sprinkle generously with cheese. Pass the remaining cheese at the table.

MAKES 4 OR 5 GENEROUS SERVINGS

SAVOY CABBAGE

Tender and mild in flavor, savoy cabbage is one of the best members of the cabbage family for cooking. Savoy cabbage has crinkled green leaves that range in color from pale to dark green. Select firm, heavy heads with closely furled leaves and, to ensure freshness, check the stem end to make sure it has not cracked around the base.

1 cup (7 oz/220 g) cannellini or small white (navy) beans

3 leeks

1 large fennel bulb

2 carrots

Salt and pepper

1 bay leaf, preferably fresh

¾ cup (2 oz/60 g) tubetti or other small soup pasta

5 tablespoons (2½ fl oz/75 ml) extra-virgin olive oil, plus extra for drizzling

3 thin slices pancetta

2 cloves garlic, crushed

1 cup (3 oz/90 g) thinly sliced savoy cabbage

Leaves from 2 small fresh rosemary sprigs, finely chopped

2 tomatoes, peeled and seeded (page 93), then chopped

6 cups (48 fl oz/1.5 l) chicken stock

Handful of fresh flat-leaf (Italian) parsley leaves, coarsely chopped

1 cup (4 oz/125 g) grated pecorino romano cheese

PENNE WITH LAMB RAGÙ AND MINT

2 whole lamb shanks
(about 1 lb/500 g each)

Salt and pepper

¼ cup (2 fl oz/60 ml) olive
oil, plus extra for drizzling

3 leeks, white part only,
cut into small dice

1 carrot, peeled and cut
into small dice

3 cloves garlic, sliced

½ cup (4 fl oz/125 ml)
full-bodied dry red wine
such as Chianti

½ cup (4 fl oz/125 ml)
light meat stock (page 111)
or chicken stock

1 can (35 oz/1.1 kg)
plum (Roma) tomatoes,
chopped, with juice

1 bay leaf

2 long strips orange zest

Small handful of fresh mint
leaves, coarsely chopped,
plus 3 sprigs

12 fresh basil leaves,
coarsely chopped

1 lb (500 g) penne or
cavatelli

1 cup (4 oz/125 g) grated
pecorino romano cheese

Preheat the oven to 350°F (180°C). Season the lamb shanks with salt and pepper to taste. In a Dutch oven or heavy flameproof casserole dish over medium heat, warm the ¼ cup olive oil. Add the lamb shanks and brown them well on all sides. Remove the shanks from the pan and drain off the excess fat. Add the leeks and carrot and sauté until soft and fragrant, about 8 minutes. Add the garlic and sauté for 1 minute, not letting it color. Return the shanks to the pan, pour the red wine over them, and cook until the wine is reduced by about half. Add the stock, tomatoes with their juice, bay leaf, and orange zest. Bring to a boil. Turn off the heat, cover, and place in the oven. Braise until the lamb is very tender, about 1½ hours. Transfer the lamb to a cutting board and tent with aluminum foil to keep warm. Skim the fat from the surface of the sauce. Add the chopped mint and basil. Taste and adjust the seasoning.

Bring a large pot of water to a boil. Generously salt the boiling water, add the pasta, and cook until al dente, 10–12 minutes. Drain well. Put the pasta in a warmed large, shallow bowl and add about 2 tablespoons of the grated cheese and a drizzle of olive oil. Toss. Pour on about three-quarters of the sauce and toss again. Garnish with the mint sprigs. Pass the remaining cheese at the table.

Slice the lamb thinly and arrange on a platter. Pour on the remaining sauce, and serve as a second course.

Serving Tip: This dish is designed to be served in two courses, as a pasta course followed by a light meat course. Serve the second course with a green salad or vegetable.

MAKES 4 MAIN-COURSE SERVINGS

FRESH MINT

In various regions of Italy, especially around Rome and in Sicily, fresh mint is used as a flavoring for meat, vegetables, and fish dishes. The mint most often used is a wild herb that has a sophisticated and mellow taste, unlike spearmint or peppermint, which can be too sharp. Blending spearmint with basil gives a flavor similar to this herb, known as *nepitella* in Italian. When shopping for mint for this recipe, pass over dark green, strongly scented peppermint in favor of milder, lighter green spearmint.

HEARTY VEGETARIAN

Vegetarian pastas are especially popular in southern Italy, where vegetables grow in abundance and meat has traditionally been reserved for Sundays and feast days. These substantial meatless dishes are tempting main courses even for nonvegetarians.

CAVATAPPI WITH CAULIFLOWER, SAFFRON,
PINE NUTS, AND CURRANTS
90

VEGETABLE SOUP WITH ANELLINI
93

WHOLE-WHEAT PENNE WITH BRAISED
GARLIC AND RADICCHIO
94

ORZO SALAD WITH FETA
AND AVOCADO
97

BAKED ZITI WITH TOMATOES,
RICOTTA, AND MOZZARELLA
98

WILD GREENS–FILLED RAVIOLI
WITH WALNUT SAUCE
101

ROASTED-EGGPLANT LASAGNE
102

CAVATAPPI WITH CAULIFLOWER, SAFFRON, PINE NUTS, AND CURRANTS

Bring a large pot of water to a boil. Generously salt the boiling water and blanch the cauliflower florets for 2 minutes. Using a slotted spoon, transfer them to a colander, reserving the cooking water. Run cold water over them to stop the cooking. Drain well.

In a large frying pan over medium heat, warm the ½ cup olive oil. Add the onion and sauté until softened, about 4 minutes. Add the blanched cauliflower, salt and black pepper to taste, and cayenne and sauté until tender and well coated with oil, about 2 minutes. Add the white wine and let it boil away.

Bring the cauliflower-cooking water back to a boil. Add the pasta and cook until al dente, 8–11 minutes.

Reduce the heat to low under the frying pan, add the saffron, and simmer for 1 minute to blend the flavors.

Drain the pasta, reserving about ½ cup (4 fl oz / 125 ml) of the pasta water. Add the pasta to the frying pan. Add the pine nuts, currants, and a few tablespoons of the pasta water to loosen the sauce, if needed. Toss briefly, just to blend. Pour the pasta into a warmed large, shallow bowl and add the dill, 2 heaping tablespoons of the grated cheese, and a drizzle of olive oil. Toss to mix. Pass the remaining cheese at the table.

MAKES 4 MAIN-COURSE OR 6 FIRST-COURSE SERVINGS

SAFFRON

The stigmas of a type of crocus, saffron is used in many regions of Italy to add a subtle but exotic flavor and color to many dishes. For the best flavor, buy saffron in whole "threads" (stigmas), checking the date on the package. Fresh saffron threads are usually a bit moist. But for saffron to dissolve completely in a sauce, it's best to dry it out and grind it to a powder. Place the threads in a small frying pan over low heat and dry them out for a few seconds. Then, grind them in a mortar with a pestle.

1 large cauliflower
(about 2 lb / 1 kg), cut into
small florets

½ cup (4 fl oz / 125 ml)
extra-virgin olive oil, plus
extra for drizzling

1 large onion, thinly sliced

Salt and freshly ground
black pepper

Pinch of cayenne pepper

¼ cup (2 fl oz / 60 ml)
dry white wine

1 lb (500 g) cavatappi, fusilli,
or penne

Large pinch of saffron
threads, toasted and ground
(far left), then soaked in a
few tablespoons of warm
water

½ cup (2½ oz / 75 g)
pine nuts, lightly toasted
(page 115)

½ cup (3 oz / 90 g) dried
currants, soaked in warm
water for 5 minutes and
drained

Leaves from 2 or 3 small
fresh dill sprigs, minced

1 cup (4 oz / 125 g) grated
pecorino toscano or pecorino
romano cheese

VEGETABLE SOUP WITH ANELLINI

Salt and freshly ground pepper

½ cup (3½ oz/105 g) anellini or other small soup pasta such as tubetti, pastina, orzo, or stelline

6 tablespoons (3 fl oz/ 90 ml) extra-virgin olive oil

3 leeks, white part only, thinly sliced

1 fennel bulb, trimmed and cut into small dice, plus handful of feathery tops, chopped

1 bay leaf

Leaves from 2 or 3 large fresh thyme sprigs, chopped

2 cloves garlic, crushed

Kernels cut from 2 ears of corn

2 small zucchini (courgettes), trimmed and cut into small dice

3 large tomatoes, peeled and seeded (far right), then cut into small dice

5 oil-packed sun-dried tomatoes, drained and cut into small dice

6 cups (48 fl oz/1.5 l) vegetable stock

Genoese Pesto (page 25)

Bring a saucepan of water to a boil. Generously salt the boiling water, add the pasta, and cook until barely tender, 6–8 minutes. (It will cook further in the soup.) Drain and toss with 2 tablespoons of the olive oil.

In a large soup pot over medium heat, heat the remaining 4 tablespoons (2 fl oz/60 ml) olive oil. Add the leeks, fennel bulb and tops, bay leaf, and thyme. Season with salt and pepper to taste and sauté until all the vegetables are fragrant and just starting to soften, about 5 minutes. Add the garlic and sauté for 1 minute. Add the corn and the zucchini, season with a bit more salt, and sauté for 2–3 minutes. Add the fresh and sun-dried tomatoes and the stock. Raise the heat to high and bring to a boil. Reduce the heat to medium and cook, uncovered, at a lively simmer until all the vegetables are tender, 15–20 minutes. Skim the surface if necessary to remove any foam. Add the cooked pasta. Taste and adjust the seasoning. Cook briefly just to reheat the pasta.

Ladle into warmed bowls and top each serving with a generous dollop of pesto. Serve immediately.

MAKES 4 GENEROUS SERVINGS OR 6 SMALLER ONES

PEELING AND SEEDING TOMATOES

To peel tomatoes, score a shallow X in the blossom end of each tomato. Plunge them into a large pot of boiling water and blanch for just 15–30 seconds. Using a slotted spoon, transfer them to a bowl of cold water to stop the cooking. The skins will now slip off easily. To seed tomatoes, cut them in half crosswise. Hold each half over a sink or bowl and lightly squeeze and shake it to dislodge the seeds, using your finger if needed to help ease out the seeds.

WHOLE-WHEAT PENNE WITH BRAISED GARLIC AND RADICCHIO

RADICCHIO

The natural bitterness of radicchio is valued in Italian cooking. Two types are now typically available. *Radicchio di Treviso,* long leafed and red tipped, is excellent for cooking. It is available at many specialty-food stores during the autumn and winter months. The more commonly seen round, dark red *radicchio di Verona* is best used raw in salads. It can also be cooked, but its taste is a little less rounded and more bitter than the Treviso variety. Either type can be used in this pasta.

In a small saucepan over high heat, combine the garlic cloves with water to cover and bring to a boil. Reduce the heat to medium and simmer until the cloves are soft enough to pierce easily with a knife, about 5 minutes. Drain well. (This simmering softens the garlic's flavor, leaving the cloves very sweet.)

Bring a large pot of water to a boil. Meanwhile, in a large frying pan or flameproof casserole dish over medium heat, warm the ¼ cup olive oil. Add the garlic cloves and sauté until lightly golden, 1–2 minutes. Add the radicchio, season with salt and pepper to taste, and sauté until the radicchio just starts to wilt, 3–4 minutes. Add a splash of water to the pan and continue cooking until the radicchio is tender, about 4 minutes. There should be some liquid left in the pan. Add the rosemary and balsamic vinegar and cook for 1 minute to blend the flavors.

Generously salt the boiling water, add the penne, and cook until al dente, 10–12 minutes. Drain. Add the pasta to the frying pan and toss over low heat to mix well.

Pour the pasta mixture into a warmed large, shallow bowl. Add the pine nuts, cheese, parsley, and a drizzle of olive oil. Toss to melt the cheese and to mix all the ingredients. Serve immediately.

MAKES 4 MAIN-COURSE OR 6 FIRST-COURSE SERVINGS

Cloves from 2 heads garlic, peeled (about 20 cloves)

¼ cup (2 fl oz/60 ml) extra-virgin olive oil, plus extra for drizzling

4 heads Treviso radicchio or 3 heads Verona radicchio *(far left),* cored and thinly sliced

Salt and freshly ground pepper

Leaves from 2 or 3 small fresh rosemary sprigs, minced

Splash of balsamic vinegar

1 lb (500 g) whole-wheat or regular penne

½ cup (2½ oz/75 g) pine nuts, lightly toasted (page 115)

¾ cup (3 oz/90 g) shredded young Asiago or grated pecorino romano cheese

Handful of fresh flat-leaf (Italian) parsley leaves, coarsely chopped

ORZO SALAD WITH FETA AND AVOCADO

1 lb (500 g) orzo, preferably large-grain Greek orzo

½ cup (4 fl oz/125 ml) extra-virgin olive oil

Salt

2 Hass avocados

2 pints (24 oz/750 g) cherry tomatoes, stems removed and halved

2 cloves garlic, minced

3 shallots, thinly sliced

1 jalapeño chile, seeded, if desired, and minced

Juice of 1 orange

Grated zest of 1 lemon

5 oz (155 g) feta cheese, preferably French (see Note), crumbled

Leaves from 6 large fresh marjoram sprigs, coarsely chopped, plus 4–6 sprigs

Bring a large pot of water to a boil. Generously salt the boiling water, add the orzo, and cook until al dente, 8–10 minutes. Pour into a fine-mesh sieve and run under cold water to stop the cooking. Drain well.

Put the orzo in a large serving bowl and toss with about half of the olive oil and a pinch of salt. Pit, peel, and cut the avocados into small cubes. (Cut them just before tossing the pasta so they won't discolor.) Add the avocados, tomatoes, garlic, shallots, chile, orange juice, lemon zest, feta cheese, chopped marjoram, and the remaining olive oil. Season with salt to taste. Toss gently, being careful not to break up the avocado too much. Taste and adjust the seasoning. Garnish with marjoram sprigs and serve.

Note: Try to find French feta for this recipe. It is usually less salty and a bit creamier than Greek feta.

MAKES 4 MAIN-COURSE OR 6 FIRST-COURSE SERVINGS

ORZO

Taking its name from the Italian word for barley, orzo is a small pasta shaped not unlike large grains of rice. It is often used in pasta salads and in soups, or can make a bed for roasted or braised meats such as osso buco. Look for orzo in well-stocked supermarkets and in specialty Italian food stores. If you find large-grain Greek orzo, it is also a good choice for this recipe.

BAKED ZITI WITH TOMATOES, RICOTTA, AND MOZZARELLA

Preheat the oven to 425°F (220°C). Lightly coat a 10-by-12-inch (25-by-30-cm) baking dish with olive oil. Bring a large pot of water to a boil.

Combine the ricotta, egg yolk, ½ cup (2 oz/60 g) of the pecorino romano, nutmeg, and parsley in a large bowl. Season with salt and pepper to taste and mix to blend.

Generously salt the boiling water, add the pasta, and cook until al dente, 12–16 minutes. Drain well. Put the pasta in the mixing bowl with the ricotta mixture. Toss well. Add the heated tomato sauce and the mozzarella and toss again, briefly.

Transfer the mixture to the prepared baking dish and smooth the top. Sprinkle the remaining grated cheese over the top and drizzle with olive oil. Bake, uncovered, until bubbling hot and lightly browned, about 20 minutes. Let rest for 3–4 minutes before serving.

MAKES 4 MAIN-COURSE OR 6 FIRST-COURSE SERVINGS

Extra-virgin olive oil for coating and drizzling

1 cup (8 oz/250 g) ricotta cheese

1 egg yolk

1 cup (4 oz/125 g) grated pecorino romano cheese

Generous pinch of freshly grated nutmeg

Handful of fresh flat-leaf (Italian) parsley leaves, coarsely chopped

Salt and freshly ground pepper

1 lb (500 g) ziti

Home-Style Tomato Sauce (page 10), heated

½ lb (250 g) mozzarella cheese, cut into small cubes

WILD GREENS–FILLED RAVIOLI WITH WALNUT SAUCE

4 cups (4 oz/125 g) mixed young bitter greens *(far right)*

4 green (spring) onions, including tender green parts

5 or 6 celery leaves

12 fresh basil leaves, coarsely chopped, plus 4–6 sprigs

Leaves from 5 fresh marjoram sprigs, coarsely chopped, plus minced leaves from 2 or 3 sprigs

1 cup (8 oz/250 g) ricotta

1 egg yolk

Pinch of grated nutmeg

½ cup (2 oz/60 g) plus 2 tablespoons grated pecorino romano cheese

Salt and pepper

1 cup (4 oz/125 g) walnuts, plus chopped for garnish

1 clove garlic

⅓ cup (3 fl oz/80 ml) extra-virgin olive oil, plus extra for drizzling

½ cup (4 fl oz/125 ml) heavy (double) cream

1 lb (500 g) fresh pasta sheets (pages 107–8)

Trim the bitter greens. Plunge them into a large pot of salted boiling water and blanch for about 2 minutes. Using a skimmer, transfer the greens to a colander, reserving the cooking water. Run cold water over them to stop the cooking and to preserve their bright color. Drain and squeeze out excess water.

Chop the blanched greens well and place them in a bowl. Thinly slice the green onions and chop the celery leaves and add them to the bowl along with the basil, chopped marjoram, ricotta, egg yolk, nutmeg, and the 2 tablespoons pecorino. Season with salt and pepper to taste and mix well. Taste and adjust the seasoning.

In a blender or food processor, combine the 1 cup walnuts and garlic and chop coarsely. Add the ⅓ cup olive oil, minced marjoram, cream, and salt to taste and process to a coarse paste. (The sauce should not be too smooth.) Put in a small bowl, add the ½ cup pecorino, and mix well. Set aside.

Using the pasta sheets and the wild greens mixture, prepare the ravioli (page 110) and lay them out on floured baking sheets.

Return the greens-cooking water to a boil, add the ravioli, and cook until tender, 30 seconds–3 minutes, depending on the freshness of the pasta. (Unless you have a huge pot, you will probably need to do this in 2 batches.) Using a skimmer, transfer to paper towels to drain briefly. Put the ravioli in a warmed large, shallow bowl. (Drizzle the first batch with a little olive oil so they don't stick together.) Reserve about ½ cup (4 fl oz/125 ml) pasta-cooking water. Pour on the walnut sauce, add about 2 tablespoons pasta water, and toss gently to distribute the sauce, adding more water as necessary. Garnish with walnuts and basil sprigs and serve.

MAKES 4 MAIN-COURSE OR 6 FIRST-COURSE SERVINGS

WILD GREENS VARIATIONS

This dish is an interpretation of *pansôti,* the famous ravioli from Liguria that are filled with a mix of several kinds of wild greens. Dandelion leaves, arugula (rocket), and Swiss chard make a nice combination and are fairly easy to find, but you can substitute any other greens you wish, such as spinach, escarole (Batavian endive), chicory (curly endive), beet tops, or watercress. The most important thing for the flavor is to have a mixture of several types of greens.

ROASTED-EGGPLANT LASAGNE

DRAINING EGGPLANT

If an eggplant is large, it may contain enough moisture to interfere with cooking, making a dish watery. Large eggplants may be salted to draw out this excess moisture. Cut the eggplant into pieces and sprinkle with coarse salt on all sides. Put the pieces in a colander set over a plate. Let drain for about 30 minutes. Spread the eggplant on a double thickness of paper towels and, using more paper towels, gently press to squeeze out excess moisture and wipe away excess salt. Do not rinse under running water, as the eggplant will absorb the water.

Preheat the oven to 450°F (230°C). Put the eggplants, bell pepper, and onion in a large baking pan and spread them out. Put the tomatoes and garlic on a baking sheet. Drizzle each pan with 3 tablespoons of the olive oil and season with salt and pepper, turning the vegetables to coat. Sprinkle the rosemary over the eggplant mixture. Roast until the vegetables are tender and just starting to brown at the edges, about 20 minutes for the tomatoes and 25–30 minutes for the eggplant, stirring once during roasting.

Meanwhile, cook the pasta a few sheets at a time in salted boiling water until al dente, 30 seconds–3 minutes, depending on the freshness of the pasta. Using a skimmer, transfer them to a colander. Run cold water over them to stop the cooking, drain well, and lay them out on damp kitchen towels until ready to use.

Remove the vegetables from the oven and add the olives to the tomato mixture. Taste and adjust the seasoning of the vegetable mixtures, adding a drizzle of olive oil if they seem at all dry.

In a small bowl, combine the goat cheese, ricotta, cream, and parsley. Add salt and pepper to taste and blend until smooth.

Lightly oil a 10-by-12-inch (25-by-30-cm) baking dish. Place a layer of pasta sheets in the baking dish. Reserve ½ cup (4 fl oz / 125 ml) of the tomato mixture. Layer a third of the remaining tomato mixture and a third of the eggplant mixture over the pasta in the dish. Add another layer of pasta and dot with all of the goat cheese mixture. Top with half of the remaining tomato and eggplant mixtures. Add another layer of pasta and another layer of tomato and eggplant mixtures. Top with a final layer of pasta and the reserved tomato mixture. Sprinkle with the grated cheese and drizzle with olive oil. Bake the lasagne until bubbling hot and lightly browned, about 20 minutes. Let rest 3–5 minutes to firm the lasagne before serving.

MAKES 4–6 MAIN-COURSE SERVINGS

2 eggplants (aubergines), cut into small dice, salted and drained if necessary *(far left)*

1 red bell pepper (capsicum), seeded and cut into small dice

1 large, sweet white onion such as Vidalia, diced

6 large tomatoes, diced

4 cloves garlic, sliced

6 tablespoons (3 fl oz / 80 ml) extra-virgin olive oil, plus extra for drizzling

Salt and pepper

Leaves from 2 or 3 small fresh rosemary sprigs, minced

1 lb (500 g) fresh green lasagne sheets (pages 107–8)

½ cup (2½ oz / 75 g) pitted Mediterranean-style black olives, halved

1 log (11 oz / 345 g) fresh goat cheese, softened

1 cup (8 oz / 250 g) ricotta cheese

½ cup (4 fl oz / 125 ml) heavy (double) cream

Leaves from 3 or 4 large fresh flat-leaf (Italian) parsley sprigs, coarsely chopped

½ cup (2 oz / 60 g) grated Parmesan cheese

PASTA BASICS

Most pasta recipes are simple enough to be used as frameworks for exploring your own culinary imagination. Your best meals will be ones that reflect your creativity in the kitchen, so feel free to adapt the recipes in this book to your own taste, substituting herbs, vegetables, meats, and fish as you like.

CHOOSING INGREDIENTS

The simplicity and streamlined nature of most pasta dishes make choosing the best ingredients and treating them with care especially important. Buy the freshest cheeses you can find, use a good olive oil, and choose a high-quality pasta. Visit your produce and farmers' markets regularly and bring home whatever smells and looks most ripe and beautiful. The results will be delicious home cooking.

BUYING PASTA

Unless they specify otherwise, the recipes in this book call for dried pasta. If possible, choose an Italian brand. Italian dried pasta, even that made by big commercial companies, is better than most brands made elsewhere, because it contains a high percentage of protein-rich durum wheat flour and has a better texture when cooked. For a real treat, try some of the Italian artisanal pastas that are now available outside of Italy. These pastas are produced in an old-fashioned way using bronze dies that extrude the dough very slowly, leaving a rough texture on the surface that gives sauces something to cling to. The pastas are then air-dried slowly and develop a nutty taste and firm texture.

The quality of commercial fresh egg pasta runs from ordinary—supermarket products with little flavor and rubbery texture—to excellent. The best commerical pastas are made in small, sometimes family-run shops. Purchase fresh pasta the day you plan to cook it so that it stays moist and doesn't have time to pick up the refrigerator's flavors. A truly fresh pasta will taste wonderful cooked and tossed with nothing more than a little butter and grated Parmesan.

MATCHING PASTA WITH SAUCE

In many regions of Italy, certain sauces are always served with specific pastas. Traditionally, Italians dress dried pasta with an olive oil–based sauce and toss fresh pasta with sauces that include butter or cream.

You need not feel bound by tradition, but a few guidelines can be helpful in pairing sauces and pastas. Bold, chunky sauces with large pieces of sausage or chunks of eggplant look better and are easier to eat when served with large shaped pastas such as rigatoni or ziti. Finely sliced tender foods, like asparagus or mushrooms, are more suited to a thin strand or ribbon pasta, such as spaghetti or tagliatelle. Julienned vegetables wrap beautifully around the corkscrew shape of fusilli or cavatappi. Finely diced zucchini nestles nicely in the rounded hollows of orecchiette. Use your imagination and taste to create your own combinations, keeping these considerations in mind.

FINISHING TOUCHES

Make sure to give your pasta or any dish a taste before setting it out on the table. It might benefit from a pinch of salt or pepper or a drizzle of olive oil. Coarsely chopped fresh herbs added at the last minute will give dishes a burst of freshness, as might a splash of lemon juice.

MAKING PASTA

Making pasta can be a pleasurable and rewarding experience, and the resulting taste will be superior to that of anything you can buy, especially when you become experienced enough to roll it out thinly. Try making pasta on an afternoon when you have some free time and can relax and enjoy the process.

Fresh pasta should be delicate yet elastic. After mixing, either by hand or in a food processor, the dough is kneaded slowly and then allowed to rest. Next, the dough is rolled out into sheets, either by hand or with a hand-cranked pasta machine. Once you start, you'll quickly learn which method works best for you.

The first step is to make the dough. Shown opposite are the basic steps in making an egg pasta dough:

1 **Making a well in the flour**: The flour well acts as a temporary bowl for mixing the egg into the flour.

2 **Mixing the flour and eggs**: Use a fork to blend until a stiff dough forms.

3 **Kneading the dough**: Push with the heels of the palms and fold the dough back onto itself until smooth and elastic.

4 **Cutting the dough into quarters**: Smaller quantities are more manageable for rolling out.

PLAIN EGG PASTA

3¾ cups (19 oz/590 g) unbleached all-purpose (plain) flour, plus more for kneading

4 eggs

Drizzle of extra-virgin olive oil

Salt

Place the flour in a mound on a wooden countertop or a plastic surface (stainless steel or marble surfaces are cold and can reduce the elasticity of the dough). Make a well in the flour and break the eggs into it.

Add a drizzle of olive oil and a pinch of salt to the well. Start beating the eggs with a fork, pushing up the flour around the edges with your other hand to make sure no egg runs out, and pulling flour from the sides of the mound into the eggs.

When you have pulled in enough flour to form a ball too stiff to beat with your fork, start kneading the dough with the palm of your hand, incorporating as much flour as you can. (You may have up to ¾ cup/4 oz/125 g leftover flour.) You should now have a big ball of dough and a bunch of tiny, crumbly dough balls that have not been incorporated. Push these aside and scrape the surface clean with a metal spatula.

Sprinkle the cleaned surface with more flour, place the dough on top, and knead by pushing it down and away from you, stretching it out. Fold the dough in half and continue pushing it down and away. Keep repeating this action until the dough no longer feels sticky and has a smooth surface. This should take about 15 minutes.

(This process is important for a delicate, elastic pasta, so don't rush.) Add more flour if the dough continues to feel sticky. When the dough is smooth, wrap it in plastic wrap and let rest for 30 minutes at room temperature to relax the dough before rolling out.

Cut the dough into 4 pieces to make it easier to roll out. Keep the dough you are not working with wrapped in plastic. See page 108 for instructions on rolling out pasta. Makes about 1 lb (500 g).

Green Pasta Variation: Add ½ cup (4 fl oz/125 ml) puréed fresh or frozen spinach, young Swiss chard, watercress, arugula (rocket), or sorrel with the oil and salt.

Tomato Pasta Variation: Add approximately 2 tablespoons tomato paste or puréed oil-packed sun-dried tomatoes with the oil and salt.

Herb Pasta Variation: Add ⅓ cup (½ oz/15 g) very finely chopped fresh herbs such as rosemary, parsley, basil, thyme, marjoram, sage, or a mixture with the oil and salt.

Saffron Pasta Variation: Toast a generous pinch of saffron threads, then grind to a powder in a mortar (see page 90). Dissolve the saffron in a couple of tablespoons hot water and add with the oil and salt.

Black or Red Pepper Pasta Variation: Add 1 tablespoon very finely ground black pepper or paprika with the oil and salt.

ROLLING OUT PASTA

Rolling out pasta by hand takes a bit of practice, but will give you a more delicate pasta with a slightly uneven surface, which is best for holding sauces. A hand-cranked pasta machine, however, also makes high-quality pasta. Instructions follow on how to make it both ways.

ROLLING OUT PASTA BY HAND

Dust a large, even work surface with flour. Place 1 piece of dough on the surface and flatten it with the palm of your hand. Using a rolling pin, preferably a long, thin one, place the pin in the middle of the dough and start rolling out toward the edge *(opposite, top left)*. Pick up the dough and give it a quarter turn. Keep rolling out toward the edge and turning the dough. Dust with flour if the dough starts to stick. You will eventually have a large, thin, smooth sheet of pasta. Ideally, it should be thin enough that you can see your hand through it when you hold it up to the light *(opposite, bottom left)*.

ROLLING OUT WITH A PASTA MACHINE

Run 1 piece of dough through the widest setting on the machine 2 or 3 times. Flour the dough lightly if it starts to stick. Fold the dough into thirds, go to the next narrower setting, and run the dough through again, then repeat this twice, lightly flouring as necessary *(opposite, top right)*. The pasta should become longer, thinner, and more even. Fold, flour, and run the dough 2 or 3 times through each progressively narrower setting until you have a long, thin, smooth sheet of pasta. Stopping after the next-to-last setting is fine for ribbon pasta; ideally, pasta for lasagne should be run through the thinnest setting. If the sheets become too long to work with easily, cut them in half.

For tagliatelle, taglierini, and pappardelle, lay the finished sheets out on a lightly floured surface and let them sit for 1–2 minutes before cutting (the brief drying will make them easier to cut). If using the sheets for ravioli, keep them as moist as possible until ready to use.

CUTTING FRESH PASTA

Cutting pasta, like rolling out, may be done by hand or by pasta machine.

FOR TAGLIATELLE OR TAGLIERINI

Tagliatelle or the slightly thinner taglierini can be cut on your pasta machine using its two settings; the thicker one is for tagliatelle. Simply run the lightly dried sheets through the setting. Occasionally, however, the pasta machine doesn't cut the pasta so that the strands are completely separated, so it is often easier to cut it by hand. To do this, roll each sheet into a loose cylinder. Using a sharp knife, cut each roll crosswise into ¼-inch (6-mm) strips for taglierini, ⅓-inch (9-mm) strips for tagliatelle (fettuccine). The general length for these pastas should be 10 inches (25 cm). Unroll the strands and place on a lightly floured baking sheet. Dust with flour to prevent sticking.

FOR PAPPARDELLE

Cut the slightly dried pasta sheets into ¾-inch (2-cm) strips for pappardelle *(opposite, bottom right)*.

FOR CANNELLONI

The hand-cranked pasta machine will give you long sheets 4–5 inches (10–13 cm) wide. Cut them into 6-inch (15-cm) lengths for cannelloni. If you are working with hand-rolled sheets, cut them into 5-by-6-inch (13-by-15-cm) rectangles.

FOR LASAGNE

Lasagne sheets don't have to be uniform. Hand-rolled sheets can be cut into large squares or pieces 5 inches (13 cm) wide and the length of your baking dish. Cut and patch as

needed to make each layer of pasta. Save a few perfect sheets for the top. The key is not the size but the delicacy of the pasta for lasagne: try to roll it out as thin as possible. It will taste better, and you will have a few extra sheets in case some tear.

FOR RAVIOLI

There is no correct size for ravioli. You can make very large or very small ones in a variety of shapes. To make large, square ravioli, roll out a pasta sheet with the hand-cranked pasta machine and place it on a floured surface. Dot the sheet with evenly spaced tablespoons of filling. Using your finger or a pastry brush, dampen the edges and the spaces between the filling with water and place another pasta sheet on top. Press down to remove air bubbles and to seal the ravioli around the fillings. Cut and trim the edges with a sharp knife. To make smaller, square ravioli, place evenly spaced teaspoons of filling along 1 side of the pasta sheet, dampen the edges and spaces, and then fold it over lengthwise. Round ravioli can be made with a round cookie cutter. Just fill and press 2 rounds together, making sure to wet the edges before sealing. Fold pasta rounds in half over a filling to make half-moons.

Ravioli are delightfully simple and quick. They may be made with any number of different fillings and, when fresh, will cook in just 30 seconds. The ravioli on the front cover of this book contain nothing but ricotta cheese, and are drizzled with melted butter and garnished with toasted walnuts, fried sage, and Parmesan shavings. Once you've tried a couple of ravioli recipes, experiment to create new combinations such as this one.

STORING FRESH PASTA

After cutting the pasta into the desired size, you can cook it right away or refrigerate it. If not cooking strand pasta right away, let it dry on the baking sheet for 1–2 minutes, dust well with flour to make sure the strands will not stick together, and loosely fold the strands or form them into small nests. Let pasta dry for about 30 minutes longer, or until it feels leathery but not brittle. Wrap and refrigerate it for up to 2 days. You can also freeze it for up to 2 weeks.

COOKING FRESH AND DRIED PASTA

When cooking any type of pasta, the most important thing to remember is to use plenty of water to keep it from sticking. For 1 lb (500 g) pasta, use about 6 qt (6 l). Fill a large pot about three-quarters full of cold water (hot water can pick up residue from pipes, which can affect the taste of your pasta). Bring it to a boil over high heat and then add salt (salting earlier can sometimes cause the water to take on a slight metallic taste). Be generous, adding about 2 tablespoons for 6 qt (6 l). The water should taste salty; otherwise, the pasta will taste flat, no matter how well-seasoned your sauce is. Let the water return to a rolling boil, then drop in the pasta all at once. Give it a brief stir to prevent it from sticking together.

Fresh egg pasta, if just made and very moist, can cook in less than a minute. Older fresh pasta may take up to 3 minutes. Usually, it is done when it all floats to the surface, but taste-test a piece. It should still be slightly chewy. Fresh pasta will always be more tender than dried pasta. Test ravioli by nibbling on one of the sealed edges.

Cooking times for dried pasta vary greatly, depending on the shape and the brand you use. Use the recommended cooking times on the package as a guide, but start taste-testing several minutes before that. It should be cooked through but still be somewhat chewy, or al dente.

Once pasta is perfectly cooked, drain it in a colander and toss it with the sauce right away to prevent it from sticking (don't let it sit in a colander even for a minute). More delicate pastas such as ravioli or lasagne should be lifted from the water with a large skimmer so that they don't tear.

MAKING STOCK FOR PASTA SAUCES

Nothing elevates a pasta sauce above the ordinary like a homemade stock. Many pasta sauces, especially long-simmered ragùs, are traditionally based on stock and rely on it for taste, but even many simpler sauces benefit from a splash of chicken or vegetable stock to help pull together flavors and create moisture. Canned low-salt chicken broth is a decent substitute when just a little is needed, for instance to loosen a sauce. But when the stock is a main component, it's best to use homemade.

The following stocks are made without salt so that they will not become overly salty when reduced. This gives the cook more control over the saltiness of the final dish.

CHICKEN STOCK

2 tablespoons extra-virgin olive oil

About 3 lb (1.5 kg) mixed chicken parts such as backs, wings, and necks

1 large onion, coarsely chopped

1 leek, including tender green parts, coarsely chopped

1 large carrot, peeled and coarsely chopped

2 cloves garlic, lightly crushed

3 or 4 fresh flat-leaf (Italian) parsley sprigs

3 or 4 fresh thyme sprigs

1 bay leaf

3 or 4 peppercorns

6 cups (48 fl oz/1.5 l) water

In a large stockpot over medium heat, warm the olive oil. Add the chicken parts and sauté until lightly golden. Add all the remaining ingredients except the water and sauté for 1 minute to release their flavors. Add the water and bring to a boil over high heat. Reduce the heat to low, cover partially, and simmer for about 2 hours, skimming the foam from the surface occasionally. Strain the stock, pressing down on all the bones and vegetables with the back of a large spoon to extract the flavor. Refrigerate overnight, then remove the congealed fat. Store in the refrigerator for up to 3 days, or freeze in small containers for up to 4 months. Makes about 4 cups (32 fl oz/1 l).

Light Meat Stock Variation: Replace half the chicken pieces with 3 pieces of veal or beef shank with bone, cut crosswise into 2-inch (5-cm) chunks.

VEGETABLE STOCK

3 tablespoons extra-virgin olive oil

1 large sweet white onion such as Vidalia, coarsely chopped

2 leeks, including tender green parts, coarsely chopped

2 carrots, peeled and coarsely chopped

1 small fennel bulb, trimmed and quartered

2 celery stalks, coarsely chopped

3 cloves garlic, lightly crushed

2 bay leaves

3 or 4 fresh flat-leaf (Italian) parsley sprigs

3 or 4 peppercorns

1 allspice berry

6 cups (48 fl oz/1.5 l) water

In a large stockpot over medium heat, warm the olive oil. Add all the ingredients except the water and sauté for 3–4 minutes to release their flavors. Add the water and bring to a boil over high heat. Reduce the heat to low, cover partially, and simmer for about 2 hours, skimming the foam from the surface occasionally. Strain the stock, pressing down on the vegetables with the back of a large spoon to extract the flavor. Refrigerate the stock for up to 3 days, or freeze for up to 4 months. Makes about 4 cups (32 fl oz/1 l).

Mushroom Stock Variation: Add a small handful of fresh mushroom trimmings or dried porcini mushrooms with the other ingredients.

GLOSSARY

AL DENTE An Italian phrase that literally means "to the tooth," used to indicate that pasta has been cooked until it is tender but still chewy, thus offering some resistance to the bite.

ASIAGO A cow's milk cheese made in the Veneto region of Italy. There are two kinds: aged Asiago is a hard grating cheese with a slightly sharp taste, while young Asiago is softer, has a gentle but tangy flavor, and melts beautifully. Since young Asiago is relatively soft, shred it on the large holes of a box grater-shredder.

BLANCHING Immersing food in a generous amount of boiling water for a few seconds or up to a minute. Blanched food is often then plunged into cold water to stop the cooking or, in the case of green vegetables, brighten the color. Blanching is done for many reasons. It softens foods before further cooking, helps loosen thin skins for peeling, and mellows strong flavors.

CHILES, SEEDING The heat of chiles varies even within the same variety of chile, so always taste a piece before adding it to a dish. If you are not sure about a chile's heat level, only add a little at a time; you can always add more later. The heat is concentrated in the white membranes, or ribs, inside the chile and is transferred from these membranes to the attached seeds. To lessen the heat, trim off the membranes and scrape away the seeds. If you want a hotter dish, leave a few seeds in.

When preparing chiles, be careful not to touch your eyes or mouth. Consider wearing rubber gloves to protect your hands. Thoroughly wash your hands, the cutting board, and the knife with hot, soapy water as soon as you have finished working with chiles.

COUSCOUS Sometimes mistaken for a whole grain, couscous is actually a type of pasta made from durum wheat (semolina). Homemade couscous is made by moistening semolina and rolling it between the palms of the hands to form tiny pellets. These are steamed until tender. Commercial couscous is quick cooking and available at most supermarkets and natural-food stores.

EGG, RAW Eggs that are used raw in a recipe or cooked to a temperature lower than 160°F (71°C) run a risk of being infected with salmonella or other types of bacteria, which can lead to food poisoning. This risk is of most concern to small children, pregnant women, older people, and anyone with a compromised immune system. If you have health and safety concerns, do not consume raw egg, or seek out a pasteurized egg product to replace it. Note that the eggs in Spaghetti alla Carbonara, page 14, as well as coddled, poached, and soft-boiled eggs do not reach this temperature safety zone.

LEEKS, RINSING As they grow in sandy soil, leeks collect grit between their many onion-like layers and as a result need to be carefully rinsed. This may be done in a couple of different ways. While the leek is whole, the white part can be slitted lengthwise and carefully cleaned under running water. Alternatively, the leek may be chopped or sliced and then immersed in a bowl of water. Let the grit settle to the bottom and lift out the floating leeks with a strainer. Rinse once more under running water, then pat dry and proceed as directed.

LEMON THYME The most well-known variety of the thyme family, lemon thyme adds a subtle citrus note and floral, earthy flavor to vegetables, meats, and sauces.

MASCARPONE This Italian cream cheese is noted for its combination of rich flavor and acidic tang. Similar to crème fraîche, it is sold in tubs in well-stocked food stores and in the cheese cases of Italian delicatessens.

NUTMEG The oval brown seed of a tropical evergreen tree, a nutmeg is about ¾ inch (2 cm) long, with a warm, sweet, spicy flavor. Whole nutmegs resemble unshelled pecans, and they keep their flavor much longer than ground nutmeg. Grate whole nutmeg on specialized nutmeg graters, which have tiny rasps and a small compartment for storing a nutmeg or two, or use the finest rasps of a box grater-shredder.

OLIVE OIL Spain, southern France, many areas within Italy, Greece, Tunisia, California, and Israel all produce superb olive oils, some green and pleasantly biting, others golden and more mellow, depending on the type and the age of the olives pressed. Young green olives produce green oils such as the ones found in Tuscany. Mature olives will give you a more golden, buttery oil, like many of the southern Italian oils. One is not better than another; it's a matter of style and personal taste.

The most flavorful type of olive oil, extra-virgin oil, is obtained from olives without the use of heat or chemicals. But even within these guidelines, the quality of extra-virgin oils varies greatly, depending on the care of the olive trees and how the olives are harvested and pressed.

Supermarket extra-virgins, usually relatively inexpensive, can have a non-descript character, but they can also be quite flavorful, depending on the producer. Small estate–bottled oils are the best you can buy. They will always carry an olive harvesting date and will give you information about the region where the olives were grown. Olive oil, unlike wine, does not get better with age. Check the harvesting date if there is one;

it should be no older than a year for the best quality. Choose a good supermarket extra-virgin or pure olive oil for everyday cooking; reserve a finer estate-bottled oil for salads and for drizzling over finished dishes.

OLIVES For information about green olives, see page 83. Black olives are ripened olives, soft textured and luxurious. Olives pass through stages of ripeness, producing the amazing nuances of colors from green to pale beige to chocolate brown to deep purple and all the way to shiny black. Richly flavored, dark ripe olives are produced in Italy, France, Spain, Greece, and Morocco. Varieties to use in pasta dishes are the little French Niçoise, Greek Kalamatas, Italian Gaetas, and the very mild, very large black Cerignola olive from southern Italy. The dark, shriveled oil-cured olives produced mainly in Morocco are delicious, but they are strongly flavored and rather salty. Olives that seem too salty can be blanched for a minute, then drained.

ONIONS, VIDALIA Pale yellow Vidalia onions are named for their place of origin in the state of Georgia. They are prized for their sweet and mild flavor.

PARMESAN True Parmesan, known by the trademarked name Parmigiano-Reggiano, is a firm, aged, salty cheese made from cow's milk in the Emilia-Romagna region of northern Italy. Rich and complex in flavor and possessing a

pleasant granular texture, this savory cheese is excellent grated over pasta. For freshness, purchase the cheese in wedges and grate or shave it only as needed just before use in a recipe.

PASTA SHAPES
Anellini: Small rings of pasta.

Angel hair (capellini): Thin, delicate strands of pasta resembling fine spaghetti.

Bucatini: Long, narrow tubes resembling hollow spaghetti.

Cavatappi: Short or medium-length, corkscrew-shaped pasta with ridges.

Cavatelli: Short, narrow pasta shaped like shells and tapered at both ends.

Farfalle: Bite-sized "butterflies," this pasta is also referred to as bow ties.

Fettuccine: See Tagliatelle, below.

Fusilli: Short, corkscrew-shaped tubes.

Fusilli lunghi: A version of fusilli consisting of long, twisted strands.

Gemelli: From the Italian word for "twins," this pasta shape consists of two short, intertwined strands.

Lasagnette: Thin, flat strands of pasta, usually with a ruffled edge, resembling "little lasagne."

Linguine: "Little tongues." Flat, narrow ribbons of the same general length as spaghetti.

Orzo: Slender, seedlike shapes similar to large grains of rice or barley.

Pappardelle: Wide ribbons of fresh pasta.

Pastina: Very small pasta shape often used in soups.

Penne: Literally "quills." Narrow tubes with angled ends resembling pen nibs.

Rigatoni: Ridged tubes.

Spaghetti: Long, thin, cylindrical strands. Its name derives from the Italian word for "strings."

Stelline: Meaning "little stars," these tiny pasta shapes are typically used in soups.

Tagliatelle: Long, wide "ribbons," often made from fresh pasta. The same pasta is called fettuccine in Rome, although the former is sometimes slightly wider.

Taglierini: Long, flat, narrow ribbons, usually of fresh pasta.

Tubetti: Short, stout "tubes."

Ziti: Fat, hollow tubes in short and long forms.

PERNOD A yellowish, anise-flavored liqueur originally made as a substitute for absinthe by Pernod et Fils in France. Pernod turns cloudy when mixed with water.

PINE NUTS, TOASTING The seeds of a specific variety of pine tree, found nestled in the scales of its cones, pine nuts are small and rich, with an elongated, slightly tapered shape and a resinous, sweet flavor. To toast pine nuts, place a small amount in a dry frying pan on the stove top. Toast nuts over medium heat, stirring frequently, until golden. Keep a close eye on them, for they burn quickly. Immediately transfer the nuts to a plate or paper towel and let them cool before using. Nuts will continue to toast, so cook them just a shade lighter than desired. They will become darker and crispier as they cool. Store toasted nuts in a closed container for 3 days at room temperature or wrapped in aluminum foil in the refrigerator, where they will keep for up to 10 days.

RAGÙ A long-simmered meat sauce for pasta. Many versions are made in various regions throughout Italy, but there are two basic versions. Bolognese ragù (see page 22) usually contains onion, carrot, celery, a pinch of nutmeg, ground (minced) veal and sometimes beef, white wine, and a touch of tomato. It is finished with a swirl of cream and is served with fresh egg pasta. Neapolitan ragù typically contains large cuts of meat, such as pork, beef, or sausage, that are simmered slowly in a tomato-based sauce seasoned with garlic and herbs. The sauce is used to dress a dried pasta such as ziti or rigatoni, and the meat is sliced and served as a second course. Other similar regional ragù sauces are basically variations on these two styles.

SHRIMP, DEVEINING Some shrimp have a dark intestinal vein running through them that is removed primarily for aesthetic reasons. Shrimp deveining gadgets can be found in housewares stores, but a paring knife does a fine job. Make a shallow cut following the curve of the shrimp's back just down to the vein. Slip the tip of the knife under the vein, lift it, pull the vein away, and rinse the shrimp under cold water.

TOMATOES, CANNED Canned San Marzano plum tomatoes from southern Italy are famous for their high quality, and they are well worth seeking out, but excellent domestic canned tomatoes are available as well. Whatever brand you choose, buy peeled whole tomatoes, not the crushed variety, which are sometimes packed with tomato paste or purée and will give your sauce an overly smooth and heavy texture.

Large cans of plum tomatoes are available in 35-oz (1.1-kg) and 28-oz (875-g) sizes. The larger size is perfect for making sauce to dress 1 lb (500 g) of pasta. If you can find only 28-oz (875-g) cans, add an 8-oz (250-g) can or 5 fresh plum (Roma) tomatoes, peeled (page 93) and chopped, to the sauce to make up the difference.

TRUFFLE OIL This oil is made by adding truffle shavings to olive oil, infusing the oil with truffle essence. A small amount drizzled over a finished dish is all you need to impart subtle truffle flavor. The oil is available at many gourmet food shops.

INDEX

SIMON & SCHUSTER SOURCE
A Division of Simon & Schuster Inc.
Rockefeller Center
1230 Avenue of the Americas
New York, NY 10020

WILLIAMS-SONOMA
Founder and Vice-Chairman: Chuck Williams
Book Buyer: Cecilia Michaelis

WELDON OWEN INC.
Chief Executive Officer: John Owen
President: Terry Newell
Chief Operating Officer: Larry Partington
Vice President, International Sales: Stuart Laurence
Creative Director: Gaye Allen
Series Editor: Sarah Putman Clegg
Associate Editor: Heather Belt
Production Manager: Chris Hemesath
Production Assistant: Donita Boles
Studio Manager: Brynn Breuner
Photograph Editor: Lisa Lee

Weldon Owen wishes to thank the following
people for their generous assistance and support
in producing this book: Copy Editor Carolyn Miller;
Consulting Editors Sharon Silva and Norman Kolpas;
Designers Lisa Schulz and Douglas Chalk; Food Stylists
Kim Konecny and Erin Quon; Prop Stylist Carol Hacker;
Photographer's Assistant Faiza Ali; Proofreaders
Desne Ahlers, Kate Chynoweth, Linda Bouchard, and
Carrie Bradley; Indexer Ken DellaPenta;
and Production Designer Joan Olson.

Williams-Sonoma Collection *Pasta* was
conceived and produced by Weldon Owen Inc.,
814 Montgomery Street, San Francisco,
California 94133, in collaboration with
Williams-Sonoma, 3250 Van Ness Avenue,
San Francisco, California 94109.

A Weldon Owen Production
Copyright © 2001 by Weldon Owen Inc. and
Williams-Sonoma Inc.

Set in Trajan, Utopia, and Vectora.

Color separations by Colourscan Overseas
Company (Pte.) Ltd.
Printed and bound in Singapore by Tien Wah
Press (Pte.) Ltd.

For information about special discounts for bulk
purchases, please contact Simon & Schuster
Special Sales: 1-800-456-6798 or
business@simonandschuster.com

First printed in 2001.

10

Library of Congress Cataloging-in-Publication
Data is available.

ISBN 0-7432-2443-4

A NOTE ON WEIGHTS AND MEASURES

All recipes include customary U.S. and metric measurements. Metric conversions are based on
a standard developed for these books and have been rounded off. Actual weights may vary.